PROVOCATIVE PHILOSOPHICAL QUESTIONS THAT INSPIRE DEEP THINKING AND DEEPER LIVING

ATLAS BRITTON

SMALL DOG PUBLISHING LLC

CONTENTS

INTRODUCTION

Have you always wondered about the mysteries of life and the universe? Has your mind ever wandered toward questions that go beyond the everyday? Have you ever thought about what it might have been like to study philosophy in school but worried it would be too hard? Many people want to know more about the bigger questions in life but, after picking up a famous philosophical text, find their eyes glazing over. Many of these texts are written for a highly academic audience and therefore use jargon or reference concepts that the average person would not be familiar with. Basically, it seems really hard to find somewhere to start!

Well, the good news is that you can tap into your inherent curiosity about these philosophical questions without having to get extremely technical. There are many ways these concepts can be articulated simply so that anyone who has burning questions about philosophy can still dive deeply into their curiosity without having to get a PhD in the subject.

On the other hand, you're also probably tired of self-help books and their tepid approach to philosophy. Often, books that are focused on helping you boost your productivity or overcome obstacles are reluctant to lean into darker or even depressing subject matter. They are designed to lift you up and make you feel good, so they won't engage with anything that might risk you losing your grip on reality.

But you're interested in the truth! You want to tap into some of the edgier and truly gripping ideas about the human condition. You want to investigate things that might be ugly or difficult but which engage your mind in a way nothing else can. You're looking for something that will thoroughly challenge you in some interesting and sometimes downright controversial subject matter but which won't scare you away with highly academic terminology and references to things you haven't yet learned. In short, you want a foot in the door to the world of philosophy—the real philosophy.

In this book, we will strive to inform you about some of the most foundational topics in philosophy today. This book takes a more accessible approach to philosophy, treating the subject as if you were an absolute beginner. We will get into some of the more technical aspects of philosophy but always with a lot of context and always in plain English. In this book, you will be introduced to the most important philosophers throughout history, some of their theories, and debates around their key ideas.

From learning all these different frameworks of thinking, you will be able to recontextualize your own life and create a more complete understanding of some of the questions that are burning inside you. The book will split the major aspects of philosophy into seven sections, each designed to give you a piece of the bigger puzzle that is the general field of philosophy. The chapters are by no means exhaustive, but they will provide a wide range of questions, thinkers, and discussions to get you started on your philosophical journey. The chapters are focused on knowledge, ethics, mortality, metaphysics, science, religion, and miscellaneous questions. This broad range ensures that you will be familiar with the main disciplines of philosophy so you can more deeply pursue these questions.

The first chapter of the book will deal with knowledge, or more precisely, "epistemology." Epistemology is the Greek word for the study of knowledge. Basically, it is all about wondering how we know things and how we can verify that what we think we know is true. The core question at the root of epistemology is "How do we define knowledge?"

If you haven't learned too much about this subject, it might seem obvious. We know things when we see them with our eyes or when a reliable person tells us they are so. But when you start to investigate how you can 100% verify that these things we think we know are true, you realize how complex the subject quickly becomes. Through these philosophers' theories, you will start to expand your reasoning around what it means to have knowledge.

Ethics might not seem like they are a part of philosophy, but they are actually some of the most important aspects. Likely, this is an aspect of philosophy that you have already partaken in. Most people have had some kind of ethical debate, ranging from who should have to do which chores to political opinions to thoughts on altruism. But ethics is more than just asking "What is the right thing to do?" Philosophical ethics dives much deeper.

It questions whether there even is a right or a wrong thing to do, how we define right and wrong, and whether right and wrong can be different across time and place. Ethicists might also question who has the right to decide or enforce what is right or wrong, touching on debates around authoritarianism and law enforcement. Some ethicists question whether morality itself is ethical or even necessary to the function of human society. This chapter will help you iron out some of your thoughts on right and wrong, refining what you believe is right and who you believe has the right to say so.

No one wants to think about death... except philosophers. Mortality has long fascinated philosophers throughout the world, but it's more than just debates around what happens after you die or assertions that you have to accept death stoically. Mortality is also the study of life, questioning what the meaning of it really is if we all ultimately have to die anyway and how we can reconcile our hopes and dreams with the knowledge that they can't last forever.

Philosophers interested in mortality might question whether death is inherently good or bad or even whether it is useful to place such a value judgment on something we cannot control. Another interesting concept that comes up in the study of mortality is immortality. Philosophers might ask questions like "Is immortality good?" or "How would you find meaning in an immortal life?" Asking questions about hypotheticals like immortality helps us better understand mortality and our role in it. You'll come away from this chapter no more ready for death but a lot more curious about it.

The fourth chapter will focus on metaphysics. Metaphysics is one of the most confusing and difficult branches of philosophy, so we have included it in the second half after you have already become accustomed to the philosophical way of thought. Metaphysics is essentially the study of existence itself. Metaphysical philosophers ask staggering questions like "How do we know we exist?" and "What does it mean to have a consciousness?" Metaphysics is basically like the brain turning a mirror on itself. Metaphysics also touches on ideas of identity and identification. It asks important questions about the ways in which we define a person, what makes their personality, and where the divides really lie between the self and others. It can be a highly dizzying branch of philosophy since it forces you to question whether you or the universe even exist at all, but it is also endlessly fascinating. These thinkers will help us truly unpack whether any of this even exists at all.

In the time of the ancient Greeks, philosophers were strongly linked to other fields such as math and science. This is why many philosophers from that era also came up with key scientific principles as well. In Chapter 5, we will examine the ways philosophical thought and scientific data interact with one another. We will discuss things like the relationship between the biological body and the soul or the mind, including the ways in which biology supports consciousness. Ideas around things like an immaterial soul versus biological reductionism will be a key topic in this chapter. We will also talk about how the brain learns and how that helps to develop our ideas about the world and sense of self. Finally, we will talk about the nature of time, discussing how hard scientific concepts like Einstein's theory of relativity relate to our perception of time.

In Chapter 6, we'll explore another major subject that has a lot of intersections with philosophy: religion. They both concern higher questions about the world and contemplate ideas like morality, mortality, and purpose. In fact, for most of history, some of the most important philosophers have been monks, nuns, and other religious leaders. This will be a highly controversial chapter that will dive headfirst into the big questions. We will be talking about whether God exists, different perspectives on theological order, and the relationship between religion and morality. Another question that will come up is the relationship between faith and knowledge, calling back to some of our ideas in Chapter 1, asking "Is faith knowledge?" We will also discuss the implications of God on ideas of free will versus determinism—does God control our actions? If so, how can we hold people accountable for their actions? To inform this chapter, we will be using ideas from various religions that all have their own interesting takes on these questions.

Finally, in Chapter 7, we will round up the chapters and explain how they work in a more practical context. We will also summarize and bring together some of the ideas from the previous chapters to help form a more cohesive understanding of all the things you've learned. By the end of this chapter, and the book in general, you will have gained a thorough understanding of some of the main concepts in philosophy.

What you will also have is something more universally applicable: a foundational understanding of philosophical thinking. Philosophy is so much more than just a collection of ideas. It is a way of thinking about the world, a method of training your brain to be more critical and ask difficult questions. By spending time with all these different modes of thought, you are actually training yourself to be a much keener thinker. Your skepticism and ability to reason will sharpen, and you will be much more comfortable with complex situations or ideas. Philosophy helps you to become a sharper, better person, and by bringing it into your life, you can do a lot of good for the world. So, without further ado, let's get into some of these burning questions!

1

KNOWLEDGE

And all knowledge, when separated from justice and virtue, is seen to be cunning and not wisdom. –Plato

E ven if you aren't a highly educated person, you probably know a few things. You know the capital of your country, you know your name, you know that you like tomatoes but your friend doesn't, and you know that the sky is blue. But *do* you know these things? What makes you so sure that all these things are absolute facts? Have you run them all through the scientific process? Have you done extensive research into them? Have you verified them at every turn? Chances are you haven't, but you still feel like you know them all the same.

This tension between what we think we know and how we think we know it has fascinated epistemologists for millennia. Philosophers have debated what the nature of knowledge really is and how we can define it. Many of them have come up with systems of criteria to determine what knowledge really is, and some of them have simply declared that it is impossible to know anything at all with certainty.

In this chapter, we will explore these very questions by looking at some of the established understandings of knowledge as well as some of the theories as to whether knowledge is possible at all. First, we will look at a major framework for defining knowledge known as justified true belief. This is one of the standard ways of defining knowledge, and it is a great entry point into the complex world of epistemology.

Next, we will pull back and discuss the question of having criteria for knowledge at all and all the problems it can cause. After that, we will discuss a well-established thought experiment in philosophy known as Molyneux's question. The term "thought experiment" will be used frequently throughout this book and refers to an imaginary scenario that helps us better envision a philosophical problem.

Molyneux's question concerns the relationship between the senses and inquires as to how knowledge can be acquired

Justified True Belief (handwritten)

through different senses. Following this discussion, we will look at how to provide proof for your knowledge and what constitutes adequate proof. Finally, we will look at colors as an important example of subjective knowledge. After considering all these topics, you will have a cohesive understanding of how to both prove and question knowledge.

▶ Justified True Belief   *Theaetetus Plato* (handwritten)

The story of justified true belief (or JTB, as it is often expressed) dates all the way back to the ancient Greeks. One of the most important philosophers of all time, Plato, wrote a dialogue called *Theaetetus*. In this dialogue, which reads like a play between the characters Theaetetus and Socrates, Plato refines his idea of knowledge and creates a solid definition for what he believes to be knowledge. This theory is that of JTB, or justified true belief. The way JTB works is by separating out three different aspects of knowledge.

Let's start with the last word: belief. When you have a belief about something, it means you think it's true. Everyone has beliefs, and if it is really your belief, that means that you treat it as knowledge. You might believe that you are a thoughtful person, or that God exists, or simply that you are a human being on earth. However, as we know, not all beliefs turn out to be true. We have all experienced being wrong about something, believing something to be true only to learn that it isn't.

For example, let's say you believed your friend wanted a copy of *Great Expectations* for her birthday, but when you gave it to her, she said, "Oh, sorry, I already have this one, can you return it?" You might have treated this belief as knowledge only to find out that it wasn't true at all. Therefore, belief alone does not suffice as knowledge. We can't say we know something just because we believe it.

This is where truth comes in. When you believe something to be true, and it turns out that it is, then you feel reaffirmed in your belief and treat it even more like knowledge. For example, you might believe your friend wants a copy of *David Copperfield* for her birthday, and when you give it to her, she says, "Wow, this is exactly what I wanted!" This would feel like knowledge because your belief was true.

However, there is a further hole in this theory. More precisely, there are ways you might believe something to be true, and it is, but your reasoning is all wrong. Let's take the birthday present example. Say the reason you believed your friend wanted a copy of *David Copperfield* was because you saw a copy of it in a bookstore placed beside another one on a clearance rack. You saw this as a sign that your friend would like the book even though the two books were unrelated and your friend was not with you. Your belief turned out to be true, but your reasoning was not logical, and thus you can't really say that it was knowledge. Most people would categorize this "knowledge" as a mere coincidence. Therefore, you can't really say you know something just because you believed it and it was true.

So, Plato came up with the most ironclad possible version of this theory, which is to have a belief that is both true and true for a good reason: justified true belief. So, to be able to say that you have knowledge, you not only have to believe something that is true, but you have to have a good or logical reason for thinking that it is true. So, taking the book example, if you saw *David Copperfield* at a bookstore, but it was on a table marked "You might enjoy these if you read [friend's favorite book]," then this would be a much better reason for buying it for them.

Even sounder logic would be if you saw it marked as "To-read" on your friend's Goodreads page. All of these reasons are much more logical and lead you to the conclusion in a methodical way. According to Plato, this kind of reasoning—one where you have a good reason to believe something and it turns out to be true—is the definition of knowledge.

But of course, a lot has happened since Plato was philosophizing in ancient Greece, and many philosophers since have been able to poke holes in this theory. One such philosopher is Edmund Gettier, who came up with certain specific situations where even having a justified true belief does not necessarily mean you have knowledge. This theory is known as "the Gettier problem." Let's take our "sound" reasons from the last paragraph and run them through this skeptical lens. Even if you saw *David Copperfield* on a table with your friend's favorite book, there are still ways you could be wrong. An employee or lazy customer could have put it there by accident, meaning it was never intended to be associated with your friend's favorite book in the first place.

Could you still say you "knew" that they would like it? And the other example—seeing the book on your friend's "To-read" list

—could have been the result of a hack or someone else accidentally using their account. There's also the possibility that the friend wanted to read the book at one time but her interests have changed and she no longer does; she hasn't gotten around to removing it from her "To-read" list.

If any of these turned out to be the case, could you say you had knowledge? What Gettier is essentially doing is demonstrating that the "justified" aspect of JTB is too abstract and still doesn't cover all the bases as to attributing knowledge. What looks like knowledge could just be a lucky guess that happens to be true. Or, knowledge of something could no longer be correct because the justifications for it are no longer (or have never been) valid. After the Gettier problem, JTB has been somewhat taken with a grain of salt as philosophers are reluctant to treat it as the ironclad theory it once was.

▶ The Problem of the Criterion

But the critiques of JTB don't stop there. Many other philosophers have identified ways in which JTB doesn't quite cut it when it comes to creating sound and concrete assertions about truth and reality. One 20th-century philosopher named Roderick Chisholm proposed something called "the problem of the criterion." The problem of the criterion is a fairly complex problem wherein the boundaries of definitions are blurred.

In essence, the problem of the criterion asserts that most statements involve predesignated categories that may or may not be accurate. Thus, if you say something like "My pet is a cat," you imply definitions for "pet," "cat," and even "my." What does "pet" mean in this sentence? What does "cat" mean? How do you define ownership? The statement might be a justified true belief, but it doesn't account for the possible ambiguity of the category. Then, defining the category runs into even more problems.

You might define "pet" as an animal that lives in your house, but then would all the spiders, mice, or flies that occupy your house also be pets? You might then define it more narrowly as an animal that you chose to bring into your house, but then would any friend's pet that entered your house be considered your pet as well? Merriam-Webster defines a pet as "a domesticated animal kept for pleasure rather than utility". However, I'm sure that dogs with the utility of detecting seizures or assisting a blind family member in navigating the physical world would arguably also be considered pets by their handlers. If you try to go down the road of definitions, you will run into an infinite chain of possible exceptions and additional definitions. This creates the problem of the criterion, which states that all knowledge is simply based on constructed categories that are impossible to pin down completely.

The above example may seem silly and go against common sense, but that's part of the point. Philosophy is about breaking through what we call "common sense" and trying to expose the assumptions and shorthands we tend to use on a daily basis. However, there are certain situations where the problem of the criterion is very relevant and starts to bring into question whether truth is relative.

For example, scientists recently recategorized dinosaurs as being part of the bird family. So now, if you say, "Dinosaurs are birds," your statement would ostensibly be true. However, a few decades ago, if you said the same thing, your statement would have been considered false. The same logic applies to the former "truth" that the world is flat, which then became a falsehood and was replaced by the new truth that the world is *not* flat. From these examples, we can see how changing definitions can alter our assertions of what is true or false. These categorizations can have real-life consequences.

Another example would be the legal drinking age. If a 19-year-old were to have a sip of beer in Niagara Falls, Canada, they would not be said to be partaking in underage drinking since the legal drinking age in Canada is 19. However, if that same person were to drive across the border with the beer in the glove compartment and take another sip in Niagara Falls, USA (where the legal drinking age is 21), then they would be partaking in underage drinking, even though it was the same drink and they are the same age less than a mile away.

The way we categorize things completely alters whether we define statements as true or false, and since categories can change drastically across time and space, you can't really ever say that something is completely true, since that category might have hazy definitions, change definitions in the future, or have a different definition in a different location. From this, we begin to really call into question the idea that anyone can ever have true knowledge because of the limitations of language and statements.

▶ Molyneux's Question

The way we perceive knowledge also has an important impact on how we think about it. Different senses, methods of learning, and viewpoints can skew our perception of things and potentially even lead us to different conclusions about the same subject matter. You can think of this as similar to the relationship between a book and its film adaptation. Even if no plot details are changed, the film still has a different feel than the book simply because they are different forms of media, and you will likely respond to one more than the other. One thought experiment to illustrate this effect is known as "Molyneux's question." This thought experiment was conceived during correspondence between the two philosophers William Molyneux and John Locke.

They envisioned a person who was born blind and had thus never been exposed to the visual world; they have played with differently shaped objects, particularly cubes and spheres, so they are familiar with them from a tactile perspective. Locke and Molyneux then questioned whether, if this person was miraculously given the ability to see and was presented with the same objects on a table but wasn't able to touch them, would they be able to identify them? What this question is essentially asking is whether knowledge learned by one sense is transferable to another. While there is no clear answer, it is an important tool to envision how the way in which knowledge is acquired might limit your ability to apply that knowledge elsewhere.

A more practical application of this knowledge would be to compare book learning with hands-on learning. Say you take a class in carpentry that is completely theory-based. You learned about the history of carpentry, all the required tools, and memorized step-by-step instructions on how to create things from wood. However, you have never touched any of these materials or tried out the instructions. Would you be able to successfully build something? On the other hand, say you had been a carpenter your whole life. You learned it from your father as a young child, so it comes very intuitively to you. You feel you could build a pair of shelves with your eyes closed and don't even have to think about the steps because they come so naturally to you. Does it follow, then, that you could write a manual on carpentry or teach a course in it? Not necessarily. Both of these examples show the application of epistemology to pedagogy, which is the study of educational methods. Learning something in one way doesn't guarantee that your knowledge will be just as useful and valid in a different context.

▶ Plato's Allegory of the Cave

Another philosophical thought experiment that is strongly related to Molyneux's question is Plato's "Allegory of the Cave" in his work *The Republic*. This is an ancient thought experiment developed by Plato that also challenges the idea of knowledge and subjectivity. In this thought experiment, there are five men who are trapped inside a cave. More specifically, they are shackled facing the wall of the cave and are unable to turn their heads; all they can see is the wall. Behind them is a pathway and behind the pathway in the back of the cave is a fire. Every day, carts pulled by horses and camels carry people and goods along the pathway through the cave.

The travelers cast shadows against the wall of the cave that the prisoners can see, but they make no sounds and can't communicate with the prisoners. What these prisoners are left with is merely the shadows of these travelers. According to Plato, these prisoners would, over time, develop a completely two-dimensional reality, perceiving these shadows as the actual physical manifestation of the travelers passing through the cave. They wouldn't understand that there was something three-dimensional and colorful passing through the cave, only the shadows. When they are released, the prisoners would not be able to recognize the travelers and would prefer instead to look at their shadows, which are more understandable and "true" to them.

Variations of this story include "puppeteers" who are holding various objects up behind the backs of the prisoners, casting shadows of said objects on the far wall opposite the fire. In the illustration, these objects include a table, chair, and cutout of a cat form. The conclusion is the same, that these prisoners wouldn't recognize a real table, chair, and cat if they were released into the world because those three-dimensional objects wouldn't be the same or representative as the two-dimensional images projected on the cave wall.

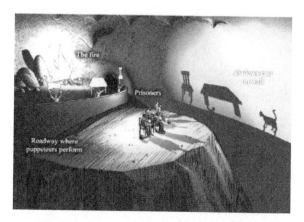

Plato's allegory of the cave. Drawing by Markus Maurer. Licensed under the Creative Commons Attribution-Share Alike 3.0 unported license.

If you're scratching your head about this allegory, don't be alarmed. All variations of this allegory rest on the premise that these prisoners have never seen a table, chair, or cat before in real life (or that it's been so long that they've actually forgotten). We can't wrap our minds around the fact that people who have been viewing 2-dimensional projections of people and objects on a wall wouldn't recognize their 3-dimensional counterparts. Believability aside, it's for the sole purpose of demonstrating a specific idea or theory.

What this thought experiment is attempting to illustrate is something far deeper than Molyneux's question. Plato's Allegory of the Cave is positing that everything perceived by human senses is merely the shadows of the real things they represent. Our eyes perceive light, shadow, and color in the world, but they can't really see the essence of things. We can see this very clearly in how easy it is to trick our eyes.

Filmmakers do this all the time, using matte paintings to look like backgrounds and green screens to superimpose actors into imaginative environments. Since our eyes only really see the surface of what's there, they can be easily tricked. So, not only do our senses not always match up in their perceptions of events and objects, but they are not perfect even when they are all working properly. Plato called this world that is inaccessible to the senses "the ideals." Ideals exist in the mind, but are not something we're able to perceive with our eyes, ears, etc. In the allegory, the travelers and objects represent the ideals—the real and true—while the shadows represent the limitations of our senses. To Plato, the senses, and therefore all knowledge, can only communicate the shadows of the ideals.

You may be wondering what this idea from over 2,400 years ago has to do with the world today. In the 1990s, scientists postulated an idea that the universe - everything we see and sense and experience in our 3-dimensional reality (4D if you include time) - is itself a hologram. In the 25 plus years since, the holographic theory still entices scientists for the opportunities it presents to resolve theoretical problems that physicists have otherwise struggled to solve. Plato and the Holographic theory stem from the same premise - that what we experience is but a mere projection of true reality. So, although these theories present a bit differently, at the core they are seeking answers to the same question!

Let's look at another example - the way that bees and other insects see the world. A bee has a very different experience of the physical world than humans, not only with respect to size and scale, but color as well. Bees have five eyes, three of which measure light intensity and two of which have thousands of facets that collect small bits of color information and stitches those bits together for a complete view. Bees cannot see the color red, but they can see ultraviolet light, which humans cannot. The UV spectrum allows the bee to discern among various types of flowers that reveal which flowers are nectar-rich.

We believe our human experience of a daisy, for example, is 100% accurate; however, we fail to acknowledge the intricate patterns and properties of the flower that are well beyond our span of ability. Perhaps the "ideal" of a daisy is the culmination of every living organism's way of experiencing it. Even then, how do we know we've captured every single attribute of the daisy? Perhaps there are characteristics no animal can see or sense.

▶ Proof

So, back when we talked about JTB, we discussed having a belief that turned out to be true. In that section, we took truth and verification for granted, assuming that it is possible to actually verify if something *is* true or not. However, not all epistemologists agree on how truth can be proven or even whether proof is possible at all. The ways in which we prove that things are either true or untrue are often subject to fallacies.

Have you ever had someone assert something to you with apparent "proof" only to find that their reasoning is shoddy?

Well, these are considered philosophical fallacies and are ways of attempting to prove something but falling short of proper evidence. One collection of these fallacies is called the "Münchhausen trilemma," named after the particularly outlandish stories told by the German Baron Karl Münchhausen. In this section, we will outline the three main fallacies in this argument and illustrate why they are not considered adequate proof.

☀ Fallacy #1: Circular Logic

The first of the three common fallacies is known as "circular logic," or "circular reasoning." Circular reasoning is essentially when you have two premises that are based on each other. So, it would be A is true because of B, and B is true because of A. Since the two are resting on each other, there is no outside proof of either, and thus they don't actually prove anything. For example:

1. You say "My professor is awful"
2. I ask "Why is the professor awful?"
3. You respond "Lots of students failed his class"
4. I ask "Why did those students fail the class?"
5. You respond "Because the professor is awful"

This would be circular logic. You have not provided adequate proof that the professor was the cause of their failure, only correlated the two things. To put it another way, the above can be stated as "My professor is awful *because* students failed his class *because* he's an awful professor *because* students failed his class *because*..." and on and on.

27

Any number of factors might have caused the students to fail, so assuming it was the professor is not based on sound reasoning. Circular logic attempts to balance two premises on one another like a house of cards, but like a house of cards, their foundation is incredibly flimsy and subject to easy takedowns.

☀ Fallacy #2: Infinite Regress

The second major fallacy is that of the "infinite regress." This is a fallacious argument that actually doesn't have any proof but continues to resort to more and more proof-lacking arguments for eternity. In letters, this argument would be structured like this: A is true because of B, B is true because of C, C is true because of D, and so on. Because the argument never reaches anything it can firmly sit on, it doesn't adequately prove itself.

One comical representation of the infinite regress is in the story of the turtles. The story goes that an astronomy professor was taking questions after class, and an old woman came up to him. She states that the earth is not round at all but is instead a disc sitting on the back of a turtle. The astronomer is surprised and amused, but being a scientist, he asks a follow-up question: "What is the turtle sitting on?" The woman responds, "Well, another turtle, of course!" The astronomer tries to hold back laughter and asks, "And what is that turtle sitting on?" The old woman chuckles and shakes her head. "My dear," she says, "it's turtles all the way down!" This ridiculous image of an infinite line of turtles supporting the earth is a perfect representation of the infinite regress argument and shows how these arguments are completely foundationless and nonsensical.

☀ *Fallacy #3: Axiomatic Arguments*

In philosophy, an "axiom" is known as a predisposed assumption about something or the world that is so well-established that there's no need to prove its validity. These axioms don't require proof because they're self-explanatory. For example, parallel lines will never cross. We know this is a certainty because of the presupposed knowledge that at any point along those lines, the distance between the two will never vary. No one needs to examine those two lines to infinity because we know what the result will be from here to eternity - they will remain separate and will never cross.

Some more examples: The sun rises in the East and sets in the West (from our perspective on Earth, anyway). An iceberg would cease to exist if it were transported to the Sahara Desert. Games like chess and poker have a specific rules about how to play the game. There is no need to prove why and how various game pieces are utilized since the validity of their moves and functionality is defined in the rules assigned to the game. Similarly, there's no need to independently validate that a royal flush is the best hand you can get in a game of Poker. We know that to be the case based on the universally agreed-upon framework of the game.

▶ Colors and Knowledge

Have you ever experienced a difference in taste? You almost certainly have. Maybe your significant other picked a movie to watch that they liked but you didn't. Maybe a friend chose an outfit that is something you'd never wear because that's not your style and you find it to be undesirable. Perhaps your neighbor bought a car that made you wonder what on Earth made them choose such a hideous color for it but clearly they liked it enough to pay big bucks for. To each his own!

All of these situations illustrate that taste and perception can vary greatly from person to person. Mostly, we chalk these things up to personal experience or preference, but lately, scientists have been theorizing that there might actually be a strong scientific basis for differences in taste, particularly when it comes to color.

Color can be one of the most subjective things around. This is why having a favorite color is so important to many people and why deciding what color to paint a common area can seem like an extremely contentious task. Scientists have theorized that this is for good reason: People might actually see colors differently from one another. What one person thinks of as blue might look different to someone else. The fact that our eyes can physically perceive colors as being different from one another actually makes a strong case for a more subjectivist understanding of the world.

Objectivism states that there is only one reality, which we all try to perceive as accurately as we can, whereas subjectivism states that everyone has their own reality. Under subjectivism, there can't really be truth because everyone's reality is different, and thus what is true for one person might not be true for another. Some people wear black all the time because they find it calming whereas others find that wearing black is depressing and avoid it. Hence, there is no true measure of objective reality. This is an extreme view of epistemology, but it allows us to see how the concept of truth can be questioned, dissected, and even challenged altogether.

ETHICS AND MORALITY

The rules of morality are not the conclusion of our reason.
–David Hume

We all think we're good people. Or, at least, we all want to believe we're good people. Each of us has our own moral code that attempts to guide us through our interactions with one another and influences our actions. This moral code might come from your religion, your politics, or simply your value system. Ethics, then, is a topic already familiar to most people. You likely started learning ethics way back in kindergarten, where teachers facilitated things like conflict resolution, fairness, and the use of words over fists.

You likely developed your moral sensibility throughout your youth, possibly even devoting yourself to a cause or disagreeing with your family over fundamental moral issues. You've probably also encountered moral ambiguity, situations where the right thing to do might not have been clear, and you were left having to hurt somebody. But, despite this fact, most of us still think we have morality all figured out. However, philosophers don't, and they have been debating some truly ambiguous moral questions for millennia.

In this chapter, we will explore some of the most important and fundamental concepts in ethics, truly challenging where you stand on many different moral topics. First, we will talk about utilitarianism, the most commonly applied system of ethics which simply prioritizes happiness and well-being for as many people as possible. Following this, we will look at a particular thought experiment criticizing utilitarianism and one of the most famous debates in philosophy, the trolley problem, which weighs the needs of the many against the needs of the few. Next, we will discuss the concept of moral luck, which debates whether reprehensibility should be measured by the intent or the outcome. After that, we will discuss the implications of free will on morality, judging whether complete free will is necessary in order for someone to be held accountable for their actions. And finally, we will talk about happiness, our perceptions around it, and when it might interact with ethics. By the end of this chapter, you might not feel like a better person, but you will certainly be able to identify ethical ideas more easily!

▶ Utilitarianism

If you asked the average person to come up with the best system of ethics they can possibly think of, then they would probably come up with something resembling utilitarianism. Utilitarianism is essentially a harm reductionist position, taking the side of wherever there is the least harm or harm for the least number of people. This system of ethics was developed in the 18th century by Jeremy Bentham and John Stuart Mill. During the 18th century, many philosophers were trying to determine measurements of morality that were secular—that is, not based on any established organized religion or associated with any concrete rewards or punishments such as heaven or hell. Thus, they had to create morality that was good for its own sake.

Utilitarianism is a position that attempts to define what is good and what is bad through inherent morality, independent of judgment or reward. There are three main aspects of utilitarianism. First of all, happiness and pleasure are valued above all else. Second of all, happiness and pleasure are equated with good, meaning that actions that promote these two things are considered good. And finally, all people's happiness counts equally. This means that something that is pleasurable for one person but causes harm to another would not be moral.

However, when you weigh the amount, or degree of harm versus degree of pleasure to make an overall judgment of something, things get blurry and must be evaluated on a case-by-case basis. In other words, imagine a scale where you place some defined "amount" of harm on one side. How much pleasure would you need to put on the other side of the scale to put the scales in balance? It sounds like a ridiculous scenario to have to think about, but we do use this type of reasoning in our lives. For example, if someone has wronged you in some way, they may ask what it would take to make it up to you. Chances are, you'll be able to come up with a specific favor that would in a way "zero out" the harm they inflicted upon you. Thus, even this fairly simplistic-sounding basis for morality is fairly complicated when looked at with more scrutiny.

So, how would utilitarianism work in practice? Let's take two examples: sex and war. In general, sex causes pleasure and happiness for the people experiencing it. Thus, under utilitarianism, it would be considered good. However, cheating on your spouse causes immense friction in the relationship since you lied to someone you love and hurt them quite deeply on an emotional level. So, even though there is temporary pleasure involved, because it comes at the expense of another person's happiness, and all people's happiness counts equally, then it would not be moral.

In the case of war, violence causes harm and would be bad in the utilitarian framework because it creates economic gains for a few people while risking the lives of many. However, one type of war that is perhaps more difficult to judge is a revolution. The French Revolution, for example, resulted in the deaths of a thousand or so aristocrats, but it resulted in the liberation of millions of people living under serfdom and likely prevented the deaths of countless peasants who might have starved otherwise.

Thus, under utilitarianism, the number of people saved might outweigh those who had to die for it. This kind of thinking is all about the "greater good," or the overall impact. Sometimes this ideology can be good, resulting in policies that protect the vulnerable from the powerful, but sometimes it can turn sour and create fascist movements. Therefore, utilitarianism can go either way and must be used as a guideline, never as a solid ideology in and of itself.

☀ The Trolley Problem

One of the most well-known challenges to utilitarianism is the trolley problem, devised by philosopher Philippa Foot in 1967. This is a thought experiment meant to stretch the boundaries of harm reduction ideologies like utilitarianism by presenting a highly simplistic version of its framework. The experiment goes like this: You approach a set of train tracks where there is a fork—one track turns into two tracks.

On each of the two tracks, there are people tied up. On one track (Track B), there is only one person, and on the other track (Track A), there are five. A train is coming and will certainly hit one of these groups who are hopelessly tied down. Currently, the track is set to run over the group of five people on Track A.

You are standing right by the track lever that has the power to change the direction of the train onto Track B so it would hit the single person instead. You don't have time to save anyone or stop the train. Your only two options are to switch the track or do nothing. So, what should you do?

A utilitarian answer in objective terms would be to switch the track. One person dying is less net harm than five people dying, so this would be the utilitarian moral choice. But if you have basic empathy, this doesn't *seem* like the moral choice. Since we all have a sense of responsibility, we'd feel more responsible for taking an action that directly resulted in killing than we would for passively letting the five people on the other track die (i.e., taking no action).

In this scenario, if deliberate action is taken to reduce the amount of overall harm by flipping the switch, it increases your reprehensibility because you had a hand in that person's death. Whereas in the passive scenario of letting the train continue on its set path, you are merely an innocent bystander and are no more responsible for those people's deaths than if you simply witnessed a car accident. From this perspective, we can see how emotional moral reasoning can actually go against utilitarianism because, in a situation like this, it feels more moral to do nothing even though doing something would reduce net harm.

☀ Variations on the Trolley Problem

There are several notable variations of the trolley problem which can manipulate your feelings about the right course of action. In this section, we will look at six of these variations to see how small changes to the details of the story can change the way you view your relative level of responsibility.

1. Direct Action

In the original thought experiment, the action you take is actually fairly indirect. You are in control of the lever, but you can choose to not be an active participant. You also are not touching any of the people involved. But what if you were more personally involved in the decision? There are two ways philosophers have illustrated this.

Number one is changing the circumstances of the singular person. Say instead of a fork in the track, you are simply standing next to someone else who has a body mass big enough to stop the train heading toward the five people. Pushing them in front of the train will kill them, but the train will stop in time to save the five people. Throwing your own body on the tracks as an alternative, of course, is not an option. Is this hands-on contact different from pulling a mechanical lever? Is it worse? Are you more responsible for their death?

The other variation is that you are the driver of the train who has the power to change the tracks. In this case, most people will say that pulling the lever is justified because the moral deniability in the original problem (of the bystander not pulling the lever) is removed. This time, you're actively determining the path of travel and are responsible for the decision either way. You can't claim to be a passive participant (or non-participant at that).

Rather, you're forced into a position of choosing the lesser of two evils: avoid hurting one person or avoid hurting five. Comparing the perspectives of the bystander versus driver, we can see how adjusting the relative relationship one has to the physical circumstances of a problem removes or adds responsibility.

2. Asymmetry

The trolley problem already presents a problem of asymmetry through numbers (one versus five individuals). However, we assume that they have equality in every other sense. Essentially, in the original problem, they are all strangers who are all going to die the exact same way and whose lives all have equal value. But what if they had different qualities? What if there were different circumstances surrounding the two tracks that might make your decision harder?

For example, what if the one person would have a more painful death than the other five? Or what if the one person was terminally ill and set to die within the week anyway? What if the one person is a toddler and the five are elderly? A number of circumstances might alter your judgment of the situation. In the next four variations, we will propose some other asymmetrical versions that might have an impact on the way you respond to the thought experiment.

3. Nonfatal

Another variation of the problem is that all people involved would sustain nonfatal injuries. For instance, all of them would be paralyzed from the waist down for life, or all of them would sustain leg fractures but would recover in a few months. Would you feel as though your responsibility was as great? Would you feel as reprehensible for choosing the one person over the five?

The other important aspect of the nonfatal variation is that the one person you chose to injure is still alive after the problem and will be extremely bothered by the fact you've forever altered his mobility for the duration of his life. He can hold you accountable and might even try to sue you in court. Perhaps this changes the nature of the problem somewhat because you actually have to confront the person face-to-face after you actively chose to harm them instead of the others. In this case, the nonfatal variation makes you less responsible since no one is going to die, but it also forces you to confront your responsibility more because all parties will still be alive.

4. Uncertainty

In the original problem, it is certain that all parties who are hit by the trolley will die without question, but what if you aren't so sure? In the real world, you likely wouldn't be, so how does this impact your decision? What if you were certain about one but not the other?

Say you knew for a fact that the one person would die, but weren't sure if the five people necessarily would. Perhaps it's foggy and you have limited visibility of the five people and it *appears* that only their ankles are bound to the track and the rest of their bodies are safe. If that's true, they'd suffer traumatic injury but wouldn't face certain death. Additionally, *if* what you see is true, perhaps one or more of those individuals could untie their ankles from the tracks. But how much stake can you put into an uncertain evaluation due to impaired visibility? What if you're wrong and they're actually fully bound to the tracks just like the one person is and will certainly die? How would the introduction of uncertainty in a situation affect your decision?

This lack of secure knowledge about who is going to die or whether they even will means that your decision-making is based on hypotheticals and the outcome might change how you feel. This connects to the idea of moral luck, which we will discuss later on in this chapter.

5. People Involved

One interesting variable is the nature of the people involved. The most common version of this variation is to involve a loved one. What if the singular person on the track is your mother, sibling, or close friend? Would that change your decision? What if there were people you cared about on both sides of the track? For example, what if the singular person was your father and one of the five people was your mother? Or what if they were two of your children? How would the moral dilemma change?

We can get even deeper with this aspect of the variation when you think about the nature of the people, even if they are strangers. What if you happened to know that one of the five people was a serial killer? Would it be worth it to let them die, along with the four other innocent people, to avenge the deaths of prior victims of the serial killer or prevent future murders?

It could also be the opposite: What if the singular person was an important political figure whose death could cause unrest or a scientist mere days away from curing cancer? All these circumstances create additional metaphorical trolley problems *within* the trolley problem. You are left guessing at the number of people that might be harmed or helped by the future actions of the people whose lives are in your hands.

6. Voluntary Death

The trolley problem deliberately does not include you personally on the tracks because it would be too simple. Most people would allow themselves to die rather than kill five people. But what if the people within the problem also feel this way and express that to you? Say the singular person says they are willing to die for the others and explicitly instructs you to pull the lever. How much responsibility do you have then? If you don't pull the lever, you run the risk of that singular person resenting you for not following their wishes and suffering from survivor's guilt, perhaps deep depression and PTSD, compromising their quality of life. However, if you do pull the lever and kill them, you are essentially participating in assisted suicide. The individual opinions of the actors involved are another aspect of the way in which harm is characterized.

▶ Moral Luck

One of the most common things about which people disagree when it comes to morality is whether the intention or the outcome is more important. In most moral situations, we view these things as the same. Either someone sets out to and succeeds at doing something *good*, or they set out to and succeed at doing something *bad*. However, sometimes people have good intentions but end up inadvertently doing something bad, or they have bad intentions but end up unwittingly doing something good.

Let's look at the following scenario: You're baking some cookies with friends, but there was a contaminant in the flour you used, which was the fault of the company you bought it from, and you end up making your friends really sick. Good intentions, bad outcome. Here's another scenario: You wanted to play a prank on your ex. You hired an actor to pretend to go on a date with them and then reject them publicly, but it turns out the actor and your ex really hit it off and end up getting married. Bad intentions, good outcome.

In both of these situations, the moral intention was inconsistent with the outcome. So, what do we do with this dichotomy? How do we reconcile what someone intended to do with what ended up actually happening? Well, the difference between these is generally known among philosophers as "moral luck," or the contribution of change into moral judgment. In the first scenario, the contribution was the contaminated flour and in the second scenario, it was the spark of romance between the actor and the ex. There's a phrase in the US about "throwing a monkey wrench into your plans" which figuratively describes what happened in both cases. In this section, we will look at how moral luck problematizes the intent/outcome disparity.

☀ The Problem of Intent

We all like to think we have good intentions, but we're faced with the challenge that intentions can be very hard to prove. Most of the time, especially when it comes to smaller acts, people don't write their intentions down or share them with others, so juries or other moral arbiters have a hard time truly figuring out a person's true intentions. Even if someone did write down their intention, it doesn't necessarily mean it's set in stone; it could theoretically change over time. Additionally, your intent may not always be clear to you or even felt wholeheartedly by you. You might want to do the right thing but get lazy or go easy on yourself, leading to negligence.

Let's go back to the baking cookies example and add a slight twist. Your intention was to bake a nice batch of cookies, but instead of unknowingly using contaminated flour as in the former example, you instead failed to look at the expiration date, which then made your friends sick.

In this situation, you'd probably be assigned more blame, even if you didn't intend to poison everybody, because you failed to take all reasonable precautions to make sure all ingredients were fresh. Therefore, intent is both hard to prove and pin down, resulting in many different intent-based gray areas.

The Problem of Outcome

So, you might say, you should base your judgment on outcome! But this is problematic as well since a person likely wouldn't deserve the punishment or reward they would get based on outcome alone. No reasonable person would truly blame the baker for making cookies with contaminated flour, and the happy couple in the second example isn't necessarily going to invite the vindictive ex who brought them together to speak at their wedding.

This is why attempted murder and manslaughter are separate crimes from murder itself. Manslaughter acknowledges the lesser crime of not intending to kill somebody (or as we say, the crime wasn't premeditated) but killing the person nonetheless. Attempted murder acknowledges that the criminal is no different from successful murderers in mindset even if the victim didn't ultimately die. If we convict people because we are afraid they will repeat their crime, then attempted murderers should be treated far worse than those who have committed manslaughter even though the attempted murder crime had a less harmful outcome. So, you really can't judge by outcome alone either.

☀ The Control Principle

Those who believe in the idea of moral luck believe that these factors beyond the person's control (the relative contamination of the flour and unexpected romantic chemistry between the ex and actor) actually do affect the judgment of one's moral character. They believe that people can be judged on outcome alone and that intent isn't relevant.

Thomas Nagel, however, would dispute this assertion. He denies that people can be held accountable for things beyond their control, so moral luck cannot really exist. He calls this the "control principle." The control principle states that people can only really be held morally accountable for things that *are* within their control. To offer an example of how we utilize Nagel's control principle to judge's people's actions, say you're at a cocktail party and someone bumps into you causing you to spill your drink. Your immediate reaction might be to blame the person who just bumped you; however, in this circumstance, that person was herself pushed by someone else rushing through the party. As a result, we typically wouldn't blame the person who directly bumped into you in this situation since she only did so due to factors beyond her control (another individual shoving past her).

In this paradigm, people are judged only by what they can reasonably control. Thus, neither intent nor outcome is supreme, simply the assessment of what a person could have reasonably known and what they did with the factors they had at their disposal.

▶ Free Will

But can we really control anything? How much of our seemingly intentional actions are actually within our control? If actions are not in your control, then how can you really be said to be responsible for your behavior? The debate over how much control we have over our circumstances is an intense one, which has implications for both metaphysics and ethics. These two positions are called "free will" and "determinism."

Free will is the assertion that we have control over the things we do, whereas determinism states that all our actions are actually the result of forced circumstances (i.e., they're predetermined). These opposing ideas are at the core of many ethical arguments and determining the level of people's reprehensibility. Here, we will look at four distinct positions on the scale of free will versus determinism and discuss their implications in the field of ethics. The scale consists of extreme freedom on one end and extreme determinism on the other.

☀ *Radical Freedom*

On the furthest side of the spectrum, we have radical freedom. Radical freedom is a theory developed by existentialist Jean-Paul Sartre. As an atheist, he argues that human beings have complete control over their thoughts and actions and therefore must be held responsible for every action they take. In other words, there's no independent force acting upon and influencing people to do what they do so people are 100% accountable for their choices and subsequent outcomes.

However, radical freedom actually moves far beyond this to the even more extreme view that we are also responsible for other human beings. Every action we take has an immense impact on the universe at large. We create others' reality and thus are not only responsible for our moral decisions but also for how they impact society. This is the most extreme view.

☀ *Limited Free Will*

The next view on the spectrum is regular or limited free will. This is the position from which most people operate in their everyday lives. Even if you believe in determinism, you still probably operate on the assumption that you have some level of free will, otherwise, it would be impossible to make decisions. However, most people also agree that there are some things outside of our control. For example, if you go to the ice cream shop wanting to get mint chocolate chip ice cream, but they're sold out of that flavor, then you cannot get that flavor, no discussions. But, outside of a few actually impossible situations, you generally have control over your life.

This position is also usually argued by people who believe in capitalism or the free market. You believe that since everyone has control over their fate, everyone has an equal opportunity to work hard and rise above their class. In this framework, people are responsible for *almost* all of their actions, barring extreme acts of chance.

☀ Circumstantial Determinism

Moving into the deterministic viewpoint, there are different kinds of determinism. This kind—circumstantial determinism —focuses on the limitations of free will based on circumstances.

So, say you went to the ice cream shop to get your scoop of mint chocolate chip, but you saw that they had raised the prices. You still technically have enough money with you, but your weekly budget can't afford to get any higher, so you go home instead. There was nothing actually stopping you from getting it, but financial circumstances were such that you really couldn't.

We can take this to another level with ethics and criminal law. In Victor Hugo's classic novel *Les Misérables*, the central character, Jean Valjean, is sentenced to 19 years of hard labor for stealing a loaf of bread. If this isn't a ridiculous enough sentence, he states that he stole the bread because his niece was close to starving and neither he nor his sister had any money for food.

Even though he did something morally reprehensible— stealing—we can see how circumstances led to his decision. In this framework, people are less responsible for their actions since there are many circumstances beyond their control that can influence how they act.

☀ Internal Determinism

Another facet of the deterministic outlook is internalized determinism, or circumstances of the mind. Those suffering from mental illnesses, trauma, or even just preconceived frameworks of thought might have just as many limitations as someone with circumstantial difficulties. Someone with an intense fear of public speaking, for example, can physically get up on a stage and speak, but due to limitations of the mind, actually cannot. Can they be held accountable for this failure? In the criminal world, there is such a thing as pleading the insanity (or mental disorder) defense. Courts will hire professional psychiatrists to determine whether the defendant was "of sound mind" when they committed their crime. Oftentimes, if they are determined not to have been of sound mind, they are given a lesser sentence. This demonstrates the perspective of internal determinism: Factors within someone's mind can have an impact on their actions, rendering them less responsible.

☀ Radical Determinism

Finally, the most extreme view on this list and the polar opposite of radical free will is radical determinism. Under radical determinism, the entire world is predetermined and everyone's actions are a result of cause and effect. From this perspective, an omniscient mathematician could theoretically write an equation to describe every action in the universe from the turning of the planets to the exact angle of a raindrop to a person's craving for potato chips. Everything is a result of physical and chemical reactions. In this sense, the future could be predicted by way of historical pattern recognition (albeit it would be unimaginably complex!). You give a computer the pattern of the past, and it would theoretically be able to "calculate" everything that will happen in the future. In this framework, no one is responsible for anything since all the "choices" you could ever make in your life are the result of predetermined factors and you as a person have zero influence over them. If this were true, there would be no point in having a criminal justice system, rewards, or punishments.

▶ Happiness

We all want to be happy, but most people feel like they really aren't. Even fewer people feel like they're happy all the time, and practically no one has never been unhappy. More pertinent to our topic of ethics: Is it morally right to be happy? Or does your moral character correlate to your happiness? We will be exploring these very questions in this section, exploring the two sides of happiness, both moral and immoral.

☀ *Virtue Happiness*

Among certain ancient Greek philosophers such as Plato and Aristotle, the dominant view was that only a truly virtuous life could lead to happiness. They associated morality with wisdom and intellect as well as personal satisfaction, thus believing that you could not be happy in your life without having these virtues. This belief is shared by many cultures and religions. Christianity, for example, teaches that a virtuous life leads to later happiness in heaven. Whether or not this means earthly happiness as well is up to interpretation, but nevertheless, it attaches a clear happiness reward for leading a moral life. The concept of karma also supports the virtue theory of happiness, asserting that the bad deeds you do will certainly come back to haunt you one day, and the good things you do will translate into others doing good for you. It's the old adage "do unto others as you would have done unto you." In other words, what you put out into the world is what you get back from it. Thus, happiness and a good life have to come from putting good out into the world.

☀ Hedonism

The opposing view is a more immediate and short-term view of happiness. Hedonism states that you should do whatever makes you feel good when you feel like doing it, presumably without any consideration for the impact on others. Hedonism also focuses intensely on pleasure—eating, playing games, sex, enjoying yourself, anything that has immediate gratification. Here are examples that fall into the pleasure bucket:

- Enjoyment
- Exhilaration
- Joy
- Relief
- Satisfaction
- Love
- Tranquility

Hedonism can be seen as a kind of "life's too short", "carpe diem", or "you only live once" mentality. It also is about avoiding things that cause displeasure. To show the broad scope of displeasure, here are some examples:

- Boredom
- Anxiety
- Fear
- Annoyance
- Isolation
- Grief
- Discomfort

Interestingly, other Greek philosophers such as Epicurus believed in hedonism. The 18th-century philosophers Jeremy Bentham and John Stuart Mill were also supporters of this viewpoint. In their view, happiness was achieved only through the pleasures, and thus an immoral life could lead to happiness. However, not all things that are immoral feel good, so hedonism isn't necessarily the polar opposite of virtue happiness, merely a neutral position focusing on present emotions to guide you to a happy life.

3

MORTALITY

Life can only be understood backwards; but it must be lived forwards. –Soren Kierkegaard

Probably the biggest question in philosophy is "What is the meaning of life?" But an equally important question is "What is the meaning of death?" Life and death, some say, are merely two sides of the same coin, and you can't study one without considering the other. We can thus condense the study of mortality itself. Humans are mortal creatures, so death is as much a fact for us as life. But how do we reconcile this fact? How do we find meaning when we know that whatever we find meaningful will end? How do we live our lives without being in constant fear of death? And what is the meaning of both of them?

In this chapter, we will dive into all the fascinating philosophical ideas about mortality, discovering the meaning of both life and death. First, we will look at life, asking what life really is and how we can find meaning in its seeming meaninglessness.

Then, we will turn toward death. In that section, we will first define what death really means and how people have tried to evade it or redefine it. Then, we will ask the question of whether death is actually an inherently bad thing or if there are some good aspects to it. And finally, we will address the question of immortality, contemplating whether it would be a blessing or a curse. In this chapter, you will encounter the opinions of important thinkers and gain a fresh perspective on the relationship between humanity, life, and death.

▶ What Does It Mean to Be Alive?

Before we can look for any specific meaning of life, we have to first ask ourselves, "What is life, really?" This question might seem like it has an obvious answer at first, but upon further inspection, it's quite complicated and reveals a lot about your outlook on the world. In this section, we will explore three distinct theories on the nature of life to help us define the phenomenon going forward.

☀ *Theory #1: Vitalism*

For those who have a more immaterial view of consciousness, vitalism is for you. Vitalism dates back to Aristotle and purports that there is a substance at the core of our beings that creates and sustains life. This is some kind of life force existing independent of our physical bodies and is often referred to as a soul. We can relate this theory of life to the concepts of the soul, chakras, or chi, which also identify a core life force within us. Basically, vitalism is the assertion that whatever gives us life or makes us conscious is an unseeable, perhaps unknowable force inside of us.

This theory is somewhat necessary for the belief in many religions since it separates the body from the soul. In many of these religions, the soul lives on even after the body dies. In some philosophies, the soul is sent to some sort of afterlife, and in others, this soul is reincarnated into another physical body on earth. Thus, this theory of life actually exceeds the parameters of life itself, the space between birth and death being simply one of the states of a soul's existence. But this ideology actually asks a lot of questions such as "Can a soul die?" and "When was the soul born?" and even "Why does death even matter if our soul continues to live on after it?" These questions and more will be explored further in the below sections about death and immortality.

☀ *Theory #2: Life as a Biography*

How many memoirs have you seen subtitled "A Life." You might see a book called *Elizabeth Taylor: A Life* or *Winston Churchill: A Life.* Instantly, we know what this means. It is a detailed account of everything that person has done. We characterize this as "a life" even though their actual life is over. Therefore, is life merely a sequence of events, bundled together only by the fact that the same person has experienced them? This theory was supported by philosopher Jay Rosenberg and is related to David Hume's bundle theory of the self. In the bundle theory, Hume asserts that we are simply the sum of all our thoughts and experiences. Thus, according to this theory, our lives can really only be characterized by the events that happen within them.

☀ Theory #3: Life as a Biological Property

Finally, we have the last theory of life, which is that life is characterized by biological properties. However, scientists haven't been able to nail down what property that should be: DNA, other genetic elements, evolution, or perhaps something else. This theory might seem like it is new since nowadays we exist in a more secular reality with a focus on biology, but it actually dates back to Aristotle. His definition of life comprised of the following: the ability to sense, to "eat", reproduce, think, and move independently. The main argument against this position is how many of these elements are required in order to identify that something is alive? Does life require that an organism has all of these characteristics? There are exceptions such as an adult silk moth, which is considered alive but doesn't engage in digestion. Also, not all organisms have the ability to reproduce. A rare disorder can cause a woman to be born without a uterus, for example, but that certainly doesn't mean she's not alive.

▶ What Is the Meaning of Life?

Now that we have some life concepts and proposed definitions in mind, we can start getting into what it means. This question sits at the core of all philosophy. In fact, it's probably the question people associate most strongly with philosophy, so much so that it's become a cliché at this point. Perhaps an image that surfaces when life's meaning comes to mind is a philosopher (or other highly trained individual) sitting quietly in solitude and pondering for hours on end among the beauties of nature. Or, you may recall from Douglas Adams' "The Hitchhiker's Guide to the Galaxy" the "ultimate question to life, the universe, and everything" was asked to a supercomputer named Deep Thought and after 7.5 million years spent calculating, the resulting comical answer was 42. But let's really get into it and discover what some of the world's most important philosophers have to say about the topic.

☀ *Spiritual Meaning*

For many people throughout history, life's meaning has been attached to religious beliefs. But what exactly do these beliefs tell us? How do these beliefs inform our understanding of life's meaning? And how do different religions represent these meanings differently? Well, there tend to be three main components of religious belief, which may or may not intersect.

The first is behavior. This is related to ethics, which we talked about in the last chapter. The second is the afterlife, or the theories and mythologies about what happens after we die.

And finally, there is origin, or the theories and mythologies around the origins of humanity and the universe. From these three components, we can usually tease out an interpretation of the meaning of life. Here, we will explore these components briefly, but we will look at them in more detail in Chapter 6, which deals exclusively with religion.

1. Behavior

Behavior is all about what we are supposed to be doing. For many religions, this is a very clear concept. For example, in charity-based religions like Christianity, Islam, and Buddhism, the most important aspect of your behavior is your treatment of the poor and less fortunate. They often have charitable donations built into the workings of their spiritual worship, such as one of the Five Pillars of Islam, which is dedicated to donating money to worthy causes. Through behavior, we can see how meaning is implied. In these charitable religions, meaning seems to derive from helping others and being a part of a strong community. From the mandates a religion puts in place, we can ascertain what their views on the meaning of life might be.

2. Afterlife

Many religions also have a theory about what happens after you die. For example, in Hinduism, it is believed that people go through a series of reincarnations within a hierarchy of living things. If you live a good life, you move up on the hierarchy, and if you live a bad life, you move down. So, if you're a person who does bad things, you might be reincarnated as a goat, whereas if you do good things, you might be reincarnated as a higher-caste person. Although ethics isn't defined in this simple explanation, we can see how they are directly related to the afterlife, providing you with a favorable afterlife if you are good and vice versa. Here, we can see that the meaning of life is making good use of your time on Earth in pursuit of a spiritual reward.

3. Origins

Finally, we can also infer a religion's view on the meaning of life through their human origin story. Seeing how they characterize where we came from can give us a good idea of how they view where we are going. For example, in Judaism, the story of Adam and Eve chronicles how humanity is inherently flawed and punishable. This positions us as people who must fight against our more primitive natures to achieve a higher or more spiritual understanding of the world. Again, the meaning of life is clear here: to rise above our human flaws and try to atone for them.

From all these religions and through these three lenses, we can see that many religions purport an ethics-based meaning of life, which tasks people with living moral existences as the ultimate source of meaning.

☀ *Humanism*

More secular versions of this religious-based mode of thinking about the world are usually focused on community and connection. This ideology is sometimes known as "humanism." Humanism is a secular view of the world that places the ultimate meaning of life on humanity rather than divine forces.

It's an early Renaissance concept that originated with renewed interest in ancient Greece and Rome in Europe. Because so many Christian scholars were studying pagan art and literature, there had to be a connection formed between them outside of religion. Emphasizing a common experience and connection among all of humanity helped them see meaning past religious differences.

To this day, many modern people use humanist ideas alongside movements of inclusivity, especially around cultural and religious diversity. The ability to find meaning outside of religion and instead within humanity itself has a few implications. First of all, it is still relatively similar to those charity-based religions we talked about where the emphasis is put on building community and helping those in need.

This is a humanist idea, so much of humanism is like religion with the God part removed. Second of all, it constructs a sort of divine human where human beings have something special about them. In humanism, humans are all equal and they maintain a special status above animals and other living things. Humanity then becomes its own meaning, and connecting and supporting each other becomes the ultimate expression of that meaning.

☀ Posthumanism

One of the more interesting movements in the study of meaning is posthumanism. As the name suggests, this movement is a reaction to humanism. It evolved in the latter half of the 20th century alongside other "post" movements, such as post-structuralism and postmodernism. All three of these movements are named such not just because they come after the movements before them, but because they are direct criticisms of those movements.

Postmodernism criticizes many of the values built up over the previous few hundred years, and post-structuralism, its sister movement, criticizes specifically those structures. Posthumanism, then, is a criticism of humanism. It objects to humanism's exclusive focus on the human experience and our perceived self-importance - even superiority - as a species.

Posthumanism recognizes that minimizing other life on our planet is detrimental to our own existence since humans, other living beings, and nature itself are all interconnected. Many posthumanists are environmental activists who claim that anthropocentrism contributes to a devaluing of plants, animals, and the earth in general. Humanism gives us a free pass to exploit the planet's resources and dangerously detaches us from our organic existence. Posthumanism supports the notion of modern scientific thought, such as recognizing that all living organisms are comprised of the same chemical elements.

For many science-based people and climate activists, posthumanism is an opportunity to take humans off our pedestal and share the earth with others.

☀ *Transhumanism*

Transhumanism describes a transformative process through which humans can surpass our natural limitations to become a sort of "post-human". Here, science blends with philosophy in that evolving technologies play a role in redefining what it means to be human, and may possibly redefine life and existence altogether. Artificial intelligence, genetic engineering, nanotechnologies, and such open the door for enhancing our experience of life, both physically and mentally.

Transhumanists support the possibility of technology improving cognitive processes, or perhaps even addressing impairments and degeneration. We may at some point identify the things that cause our bodies to age and slow down - or even stop these processes - which will allow us to live longer. These capabilities sound like science fiction as of the writing of this book, but with the speed of advances in science, these ideas may "come to life", so to speak, sooner than we may anticipate.

In today's age, we're already somewhat blurring the lines of the human body and mechanics. Consider the sleek prosthetics called running blades that allow people who would otherwise be wheelchair-bound to get around unencumbered. Some compete against the most elite athletes in the world. There have even been suggestions that these devices provide an advantage over human legs (although that assertion was disproven).

☀ Nihilism

The final type of meaning we have on this list is simply the lack of meaning. This perspective is called "nihilism." Nihilism is the belief that there is no actual meaning to life at all. Interestingly, there are very few actual proponents of nihilism. For most of modern history, nihilism has been a criticism launched at other ideologies. It is somewhat like fascism nowadays. No one would ever call themselves a fascist, but many people call other people or governments fascist. During the Enlightenment period of the 17th and 18th centuries, many philosophers would accuse one another of spouting nihilist ideology. Nihilism is often associated with German philosopher Friedrich Nietzsche; however, he, too, hated nihilism and despaired that the world was sinking into nihilist ideology.

There is one movement, however, that is nihilism-adjacent: skepticism. The skeptics, who would self-identify as such, deny the idea of absolute truth, taking a subjectivist approach to reality. For this reason, skepticism has sometimes also been called "epistemological nihilism," or nihilism of knowledge. Nietzsche was a skeptic, believing that there was no meaning in the world other than the meaning that we give it. Skepticism is interesting to pair with nihilism since it is also doubtful of meaning. However, because skepticism is more in the sphere of epistemology, it avoids the assertion that all life has no meaning at all.

From all these attitudes, we can see that humanity has come up with a wide variety of meanings for life, ranging from charitable meanings to none at all.

▶ What Is Death?

Now that we've looked at the meaning of life, we must turn to the meaning of death. Death is something none of us want to think about but has an instrumental impact on our daily lives. Many cultures have had very interesting views on death throughout history. In fact, you can tell a lot about a culture from the way they treat death. Some anthropologists even consider ceremonial burial of the dead (such as in graves with jewelry or other ritual indicators) to be an important mark of early civilizations. The way we treat and think about death has not only a strong impact on us individually, but it can actually characterize entire cultures. A question that can be asked alongside "What is the meaning of life?" and that is perhaps even more interesting is "What is the meaning of death?" Here, we are going to look at the way that cultures around the world have characterized death.

☀ *What Does It Mean to Die?*

This seems like an obvious question. You are dead when you stop breathing, when your heart stops beating, or there are no more signals in the brain. Some definitions, such as the one officially adopted by the United States from the Uniform Determination of Death Act (UDDA), state that these stops to the function of the heart, lungs, and brain must be "irreversible" (Luper, 2019). This is a scientific definition, but what about the nonscientific answer? What does it mean to be dead in practice?

For example, what do we do with people who are stuck in irreversible comas but are still breathing and having brain activity? Yes, they are still alive in medical terms, but for their friends and family, who will never talk to them or feel their presence again, isn't their date of death really the day they went into the coma?

What about individuals who suffered a traumatic event, say a major accident or cardiac arrest and were declared dead after failed attempts to revive said individuals? This sounds irreversible, but nonetheless they came back to life. Nonsense, you say? This was considered enough of a problem that in 1829, Dr Johann Gottfried Taberger invented the security coffin which contained a rope that someone who was accidentally buried alive could pull to ring a bell above ground for all to hear. Ancient history, you say? More recently, in 2014, the body of a Walter Williams of Mississippi arrived in a body bag at the funeral home where his body was to be embalmed. The coroner saw Williams' legs move; sure enough, he was alive, although he died (again) after two weeks' time.

With more thought experiments, we can muddy the water even further. What about Alzheimer's patients who might not remember their friends and family or even who they are? The experience of having a relationship with that person, sharing memories, and creating more memories together is gone. Many people who are close to those with extreme or late-stage Alzheimer's will report feeling like their loved one is gone with a stranger in their place. Is that death? Or is the fact that they can breathe, talk, and eat enough to categorize them as alive?

Another interesting perspective on death is loss of contact. You will sometimes hear someone say the phrase "They are dead to me." What this usually means is that they have chosen to cut contact with the person and operate as if they are no longer alive. Obviously, that person is still alive, being in the world and interacting with others, but to the other person, they are no longer on the earth. *Well,* you might be thinking, *in that situation, you could still contact them if you really wanted to, so it's not like they are actually dead.* In that case, let's look at another thought experiment.

Let's say there was a couple who got married in 1940, but unfortunately, the husband was drafted into World War II just a year into their marriage. They said a heartfelt goodbye, and he sailed off to France. They wrote throughout the next two years, but then one day she received a telegram saying he had died. She was devastated, but over the next few years, she processed her grief and eventually remarried.

But she was not aware that he was not dead at all but had deserted. He found a town to live in, changed his name, learned the local language, and eventually remarried someone else as well. From the wife's perspective, and the perspective of the official record, he is dead, even though in reality he is still living in the world. She will never see or speak to him again, even if she wanted to, so for all intents and purposes, he no longer exists. Is this a sort of death, just like the person in the coma? Or because he is able to interact with some people, does that simply make her wrong about his living status?

From these examples, we can see how the status of someone's physical, mental, or legal state can blur the lines between death and simply a changed state. It shows us what activities are required for us to categorize something as life. So, most people would categorize the coma example as a kind of death, especially if it was certainly irreversible, but most people would not categorize the war example as death, since the man goes on to do things and interact with people.

These examples show that most people would probably cate-gorize basic qualities such as eating, talking, walking around, and being mentally present as things you have to be able to do to at least a certain extent in order to be considered alive. The Alzheimer's example is interesting since many people with even severe Alzheimer's can still function physically, yet some people would still categorize them as "dead" in a way. Let's put it another way.

Who would you consider to be more alive: a person who is completely paralyzed but perfectly mentally sound and can communicate by blinking or someone who is perfectly physi-cally fit but catatonic and unable to communicate at all? Prob-ably the former, meaning that most people associate brain activity or the ability to communicate with others and think clear thoughts as the most important qualifier of life and the inability to do so, especially irreversibly, as an indication of death regardless of vitals.

☀ The Afterlife

The pertinent question about death is always "Does our consciousness end?" The debate around whether we continue to think or "live" in some way after we die, even if not in a body or with the same memories, has been at the core of death discussions since the beginning of humanity. Some people feel that consciousness contains a soul that will go on no matter what happens to the body, whereas others feel that when they die, that will be it for their consciousness. These tend to be the religious and nonreligious interpretations, but they grow complicated when we get into which religion we are talking about. Here, we will look at the three main versions of the afterlife (or lack thereof) in popular consciousness.

1. Heaven and Hell

In some religions, there is a paradisiacal world that some people reach when they die. For some religions, this is based on your merit as a person (such as Christianity or Islam), and if you do not pass the test, you go to a bad place, such as hell. This system is interesting since it places extra emphasis on actions throughout your life yet also diminishes life on Earth when compared to an eternal paradise. One's actions in that paradise don't matter, so the relatively small amount of time that you were on Earth is unevenly weighted.

Interestingly, the ancient Greeks did not have a heaven, only an afterlife called the underworld where everyone would go indiscriminately. The ancient Egyptians also had a vision of the underworld where the dead would keep many of their belongings after they passed, which is why Pharaohs were buried with all of their riches. These versions of the afterlife, regardless of their quality, are infinite and thus construct a reality where people live much longer in the afterlife than in real life. From the perspective of these religions or ideologies, the consciousness does not end.

2. Biological Reductionism

Those who subscribe to a view known as "biological reductionism" believe that all activities of the mind are purely systems of biology and chemistry. Whatever we call the soul is simply the complex work of brain cells. For these people, there is no afterlife but merely a blunt end. From their perspective, there was no consciousness before birth and there will be none after death. These people believe that consciousness can and does end.

3. Reincarnation

One interesting idea about continuing consciousness is reincarnation. Because reincarnation involves the reintroduction of your consciousness into another life on Earth, it is not quite an afterlife, not quite a death, and not quite immortality. Another interesting question about reincarnation from a philosophical point of view is how it affects the existence of the self. When we discussed the theory of life as a biography, we talked about Hume's bundle theory of the self which states that our selves are defined by the sum of experiences we have throughout our lives. So, if reincarnation erases our memories every time we are reborn, what makes us the same self? If you don't remember your past lives, then how do they truly impact who you are? Is the death you experience in each reincarnation cycle comparable to the death you might experience with amnesia?

There are many reported cases of young children who vividly recall living a prior life as someone else. Many even remember details about their former self's death and may have resulting trauma. If the former self died in a plane crash, for example, the chid may have a paralyzing fear of getting onto an airplane even if the child has never boarded one in their current life. Do we consider this a single continuum of one "self" or is the child a new self entirely? The prior and current incarnations certainly have different characteristics, personalities, environments, etc so what is truly connecting the two - memories?

☀ *Resurrection*

In some cultures or mythologies, resurrection is presented as a good thing, such as in Christianity. Jesus was resurrected, creating the miracle that is the basis for the entire religion. In Christianity, Jesus' resurrection was a miracle, representing His divinity and metaphorically the new beginning of humanity's relationship with God. The Easter holiday is connected closely with this episode in the Bible but also with the season of spring, which is often viewed as a natural sort of resurrection or re-awakening. We think of it as a rebirth, a time full of hope. According to Christian mythology, resurrection is good and can provide genuine new opportunities for life after death.

But in many other mythologies, resurrection is presented as something terrible or unnatural. For example, the Greek mythological figure Asklepios was killed by Zeus for resurrecting the dead because Zeus deemed it unnatural. This perspective on resurrection states that there is something inherently disturbing about the raised dead. We often see representations of this perspective in the modern zombie genre, which presents resurrection as something disgusting and scary.

Another popular culture example is in George R.R. Martin's novel *A Game of Thrones*, where Daenerys asks a witch to resurrect her dead husband. However, after the resurrection has happened, he is not himself, unable to speak or really respond. She realizes that what she asked for was unnatural and impossible and has to kill him out of mercy. From this story, we can see how life after resurrection is depicted as a sort of half-life, not really living. After someone has been sent to the world of the dead, they can't really come back whole again. Between these two vastly different depictions of resurrection, we can see a diametric opposition about the relative naturalness of death's permanence.

☀ *Immortality*

Many stories have been told about immortality. Various gods in many religions are considered to be immortal, but what about human immortality on Earth? The question of whether you would actually want to be immortal or not is something that has plagued many people because there is not an easy answer to the question. On one hand, having more time sounds great. You could pursue lots of interests, meet interesting people, and be witness to history. But on the other hand, many people feel like they would get bored, having tried everything there is to try, or that life would lose its meaning because their loved ones would all pass away in time.

Sometimes, stories about immortality depict the body decaying, but others depict it staying in a perfect state forever. One of the best ways to look at people's attitudes toward immortality is through the mythological creature of the vampire. Vampires are generally immortal, but they are also somewhat corpse-like. Depending on the mythology, they might not be able to eat real food, feel genuine love, or even be seen in a mirror. Through this mythology, we can see that many people, perhaps unconsciously, view immortality as a sort of half-life.

You get to live forever, but you are not really living. Perhaps on some level, this is a way of expressing that death is actually part of what makes us human.

Outside the realm of human beings, we know of an aptly-named animal on our planet that's considered immortal - the immortal jellyfish. When it "dies", the cells within the jelly-fish's body actually come back together into the form of a polyp, which is an earlier stage of a jellyfish's development. These polyps clone themselves and the result is multiple jelly-fish which emerge from these polyps. To scientists, this appears to be a never-ending continuation of an organism's existence by reverting to an earlier "baby" stage of develop-ment and starting the aging process anew.

▶ Death, Funeral, and Burial Rituals

One of the best ways to observe a culture's perspective on death and the dead is to see how burial and funeral rituals are done. In some cultures, funerals are a sad affair. People wear black—or white, depending on the culture's color symbolism —and will often cry, exchange sorrowful words about the person, and give each other emotional support through their grief.

However, other cultures might have a funeral that celebrates the person's life, making it more of a celebration centered around food, dancing, and good memories. Both of these perspectives can be seen as equally respectful and have one key thing in common: honoring the person who has died with some kind of ritual. Across world cultures, we can see many different practices surrounding funerals, burial, and even death itself. Here, we will look at some notable cultural perspectives on death rituals that complicate the contemporary Western attitude toward death.

☀ *Death Ritual: Yoruba Ritual Suicide*

In his play, *Death and the King's Horseman*, Nigerian author Wole Soyinka depicts a historical event surrounding a ritual suicide that took place in the early 20th century in Nigeria. In the Yoruba culture, which the story is depicting, there is a tradition where once the king dies, his horseman must commit suicide along with him in order to help transport the king into the next life. In the story, the community is getting ready to perform this death/funeral ritual when they are apprehended by the British colonial rulers. Because the British are Christians, who believe that suicide is always bad, they do not allow this ceremony to take place and even go so far as to imprison the people who are taking part in it.

Here, we can see how differing attitudes toward death and the afterlife can greatly affect the way cultures respond to it. In Christian culture, people who commit suicide are sent to hell where they are punished for a deed considered to be shameful. However, in Yoruba culture, the suicide of the horseman is considered to be honorable, like dying in battle, so he is rewarded. The Yoruba also believe in reincarnation, so death is not treated with the same permanence as in Christianity. Through these two perspectives, we can see that the way a culture assigns honor can greatly influence their attitude toward death.

☀ Funeral Ritual: *Día de los Muertos*

A tradition dating back to the Aztecs of 3,000 years ago, modern-day people in Mexico still celebrate *Día de los Muertos*, or Day of the Dead. This is a holiday that happens on the night of October 31 into November 1. On this night, the souls of the dead are said to return to the land of the living to socialize with their living family members. In practice, people will treat the event as if their deceased loved ones are really coming to visit by cooking their favorite foods, playing their favorite music, etc. It's a way to remember people by revisiting the things they surrounded themselves with when they were alive, evoking those memories and keeping the feeling of their presence alive. Though this is not a funeral per se, since it happens every year, it is still an interesting perspective on the relationship between the living and the dead and how the dead should be honored on an ongoing basis.

☀ Burial Ritual: *Toraja Preservation*

Burial, or general disposal of bodies, is another important cultural signifier. The way a body is treated after death says a lot about how that culture feels about the physical death of the body and the spiritual death of the person. In most cultures, desecrating a burial ground or not burying someone properly is considered a terrible taboo.

For example, in the ancient Greek play *Antigone*, two young soldiers desert their battalion. As punishment, they are executed, but to add insult to injury, their bodies are not buried but left to rot in the town square as an example. Their sister, Antigone, takes it upon herself to give them a proper burial in order to give their bodies the honor she believes they deserve. In the process, she risks execution herself for disobeying the king. From this story, we can see how important an honorable burial is for people who have passed and how a dishonorable burial can be seen as an enormous sign of disrespect.

However, there is one interesting culture that does not bury, burn, or dispose of the bodies in any way. The Toraja people of Indonesia actually keep the bodies of their dead loved ones in the house for long periods of time, sometimes even years. The philosophy behind this is that "a dead person who is at home is not dead" (Young, n.d.). From this, we can see that their philosophy does not equate the physical death of the body with the spiritual death of the mind as almost every other culture on Earth does.

Instead, the Toraja people continue to dress, feed, and associate with the body, prolonging their life in a sense after they have stopped breathing. Another interesting phenomenon is that the length of time the body is kept directly corresponds to the class of the family, with lower-class families keeping their bodies for only a couple of weeks and upper-class families keeping them for years on end.

From the Toraja culture, we can see an example of a people that separates spiritual death from physical death, believing that people can continue to have an experience on Earth even after their bodies have died. Not only do they continue to have an experience, the ongoing engagement by family members keeps that person an active participant in their family's everyday lives.

☀ *Burial Rituals: Native American*

There are over 570 Native American tribes and/or villages in the United States and there are many variations in the treatment of the body after death. Some tribes paint the faces of the dead the color red which symbolizes life, while others cleanse the body with yucca pre-burial. Some tie feathers around the deceased's head as a prayer offering, while others fully adorn the body head to toe and even include a pair of moccasins for the deceased to be able to travel comfortably to the next world.

One theme all Native American tribes hold in common, though, is the view that death is a natural part of the life cycle and that the souls of the deceased continue their journey thereafter. Another common belief is that the body and burial of the deceased is considered sacred. The key differentiating factor among the tribes is whether death is to be feared or accepted, and this impacts how a body is handled upon death.

The Navajo tribe, for instance, believes that ghosts of the deceased can haunt the living and precautions must be taken accordingly. This includes not leaving footprints at the site of the burial (so the ghost can't follow them back home) and refraining from displaying intense emotion when someone dies as this may disrupt the spirit's journey to the next world and the spirit might get stuck, or attached, to the physical world or even directly to a person.

In contrast, the Sioux tribe welcomes ancestral spirits to be present among the living. Members of the tribe reach out and communicate with the spirits of their ancestors to provide support during times of need. The Lakota similarly do not fear death and believe that the spirit of the deceased goes to the next world where it no longer experiences pain and suffering. There is less mourning and more celebration for the spirit's ongoing journey.

▶ Is Death Bad?

The final question we will explore in this section is a controversial one. If you ask the average person if death is a good thing or if they want to die, you will more than likely get a resounding "no." But are there some circumstances where death could actually be considered a good thing? After all, many people would consider immortality to be a bad thing, but the same people wouldn't necessarily call death good either. People who are suicidal, either because of mental health issues or terrible circumstances like terminal illnesses, might actually welcome death as a relief from their pain. As Hamlet himself said:

> *To die—to sleep,*
> *No more; and by a sleep to say we end*
> *The heart-ache and the thousand natural shocks*
> *That flesh is heir to.*
> *(William Shakespeare, 1602)*

Is Hamlet right? Is death merely a welcome end to the often painful events of life? This debate is central to the controversial topic of euthanasia, or assisted suicide. When is it okay to help someone die painlessly? Some people will say never, that it is always unethical to kill someone. However, this depends on the premise that death is always worse than any other circumstances under which a person may be living. But is this always the case?

Think back to our discussion about the trolley problem. What if you could end someone's pain but it meant killing them? It's kind of like a one-person trolley problem. For example, say someone has a terminal illness that causes them great pain. They have one month to live, but during that month their pain is going to significantly increase, culminating in an extremely painful death. The patient wants to instead die a painless death through euthanasia even though they would be cutting their life short. If there is no chance of recovery or pain reduction, wouldn't this be a better option? Some people might even want to do this if they are sentenced to life in prison because, to them, it would be preferable to a life in captivity. Luckily, Hamlet has thoughts on this:

> *[Who would] grunt and sweat under a weary life,*
> *But that the dread of something after death,*
> *The undiscovered country, from whose bourn*
> *No traveler returns, puzzles the will,*
> *And makes us rather bear those ills we have*
> *Than fly to others that we know not of?*
> *(William Shakespeare, 1602)*

The fact that, no matter your beliefs, we don't know for certain what happens after we die makes this a rather difficult trolley problem. Because we don't know where that person is going or what they might endure, it is a false choice. You are choosing between pain and the unknown, which might contain more or less pain. In essence, the choice to allow someone in pain to die peacefully is impossible because one of the variables is too great to really quantify. Some people even believe that the soul actually leaves the body immediately before a particularly horrific and intensely painful death, meaning that the departed actually doesn't experience any pain.

This is the core of the debates around euthanasia and the question of whether death is good or bad. We simply do not know since there is no scientifically researched, tested, and documented information about what death is actually like. As Hamlet said, it is a place from which "no traveler returns," making all characterization of death and its qualities pure speculation.

METAPHYSICS

Metaphysics is a dark ocean without shores or lighthouses, strewn with many a philosophic wreck. –Immanuel Kant

The fourth major branch of philosophy we will be touching on is metaphysics. Metaphysics is essentially the study of existence itself. While in the previous three chapters we focused on specific aspects of exis-

Why the world moves

tence, such as knowledge, ethics, and mortality, here we will focus on existence itself. We will be asking questions such as "What is the difference between something and nothing?" and "What is the substance of the universe?". The term "meta-physics" comes from the prefix *meta-* meaning "after" or "beyond" and the noun *physics* meaning the physical properties of the universe. Thus, metaphysics is the study of the forces that underpin our universe. However, unlike physics, which asks *how* the world moves, metaphysics asks *why* the world moves. It can be a confusing topic and much more open-ended and abstract than many of the other topics we've talked about, but it is also one of the most interesting.

In this chapter, we will explore some of the most foundational aspects of metaphysics. First, we will look at the relationship between being and nothingness. We will discuss how meta-physicians have defined the principles of reality and, more importantly, how they have deconstructed it. After that, we will talk about existence and reality in relation to the self. We will discuss different frameworks of selfhood and the implications they have on metaphysics. From these topics, you will start to gain a stronger sense of how metaphysicians look at the world and reality itself.

▶ Why Is There Something Rather Than Nothing?

One of the topics that most fascinates metaphysicians is the concept of something versus nothing. Or, put more plainly, what is the difference between something being there and not being there? Is there such a thing as *nothing*? How do we know that we, or the universe, are actually *something?* These might seem like very strange questions, but once you get into the theories of what they mean, you will be able to understand them more thoroughly.

What metaphysicians are really looking at is the fabric of reality itself. They are trying to understand the nature of things like thoughts, the senses, and material reality as well as the relationships between these things. This field is quite closely related to epistemology in the sense that you must doubt everything you know, even your senses and your own thoughts. To a metaphysician, nothing exists for certain, and thus, in a metaphysical argument, you cannot take anything for granted. In this section, we will look at different ways metaphysicians have categorized and explored nothingness and somethingness.

☀ *Nothingness*

What does it mean for there to be *nothing?* This might seem like an obvious question. You might think, *Well, nothing is the absence of something.* But what do we categorize as "something"? You might say you have "nothing to wear" even though you have a closet full of clothes. You might say that you are doing nothing even though you're sitting in a chair, breathing, and so on. You might even say that there's nothing in your hands even though there's air.

There are many ways people can use the word "nothing," often to mean the absence of what they consider to be something. So, when you say you have "nothing" to wear, what you really mean is that you have nothing you want to wear, the "something" being an outfit you are interested in and the "nothing" being the absence of that. When you say you are doing "nothing," what you really mean is that you are not partaking in any active activities, which is your definition of "something" at that moment. Saying that there is "nothing" in your hands really means that there isn't anything of mass that you can see, air being so ubiquitous that it is negligible in your life and thus doesn't qualify as "something." As we can see, these subjective definitions of "something" can really modify our definition of "nothing."

Okay, so colloquially, we might use the word "nothing" to metaphorically mean the absence of something we consider to be of substance or importance. But what actually is "nothing"? Most of the earth is taken up by either air or water, so hardly anyone on Earth has ever experienced a physical space without matter all around. But what about space? What about in a vacuum where there is no air or gasses of any kind? Is that nothing?

According to physicists and chemists, a vacuum would be considered nothing, but metaphysicians might not necessarily agree. Even the fact that we have a name for it means that it is not *nothing*. Besides, a vacuum can be contained in something. If you suck all the air out of a box, you might still consider it to be a box or even the inside to be "the contents of that box." The other quality of this version of "nothing," or a vacuum, that makes its status dubious is that it can always be filled with something at any moment, making its status as nothing constantly in flux. If light is passing through the vacuum, does that qualify as "something"? There is no fixed area of the universe where "something" could not be.

Thus, a vacuum can't truly be said to be "nothing" in the philosophical sense because it is still empty space where there is the potential to be something. Also, "empty space" is a label, so it must be labeling *something*. Does empty space thus qualify as "something"? How, then, can we say there was "nothing" before the Big Bang or that there is "nothing" after the boundary of the universe? As a thought experiment, let's say the universe exists inside a vacuum. If the universe is said to be expanding outward, then there must be some kind of nothingness that actually prevents somethingness from entering (until the somethingness reaches that "edge" of nothingness).

The trouble with picturing this kind of nothingness is that we don't have a reference point. A vacuum works fairly similarly to air, so we can simply picture it as if we were in an air-filled room, only with no air resistance (and arguably, no light). But a kind of nothingness that does not allow somethingness to enter, that is opaque in a way yet contains no matter, is next to impossible for humans to envision. We must have some version of nothingness that goes beyond a simple vacuum.

There are aspects of nothingness that, because we are made of something, we cannot possibly conceive. What does nothingness look and feel like? Does it have attributes that can be defined? Paradoxically, we also have difficulty perceiving a universe that is infinite, which is to say there's an absence of a boundary between something and nothing. An infinite universe has no nothingness because there is something every-where, in all directions, forever.

The idea of nothingness—the boundary of the universe—has boggled metaphysicians, representing the boundary between something and nothing. There are a few metaphysical suggestions for what could exist beyond the boundary of the universe, all of which seem to be paradoxical. One theory is the universe ends at some point—both matter and the possibility for matter to enter—but what lies outside of it? An opaque nothingness? Another theory posits that the universe is expanding, somethingness expanding itself into nothingness. A third theory asserts that the universe is circular in some way, similar to a sphere. Just as the surface of the earth is an infinite two-dimensional plane mapped onto a three-dimensional one, the universe could be an infinite three-dimensional plane mapped onto a four-dimensional one. But again, what lies outside of that sphere? As long as there is a finite amount of matter, there must be an amount of nothingness, no matter how difficult it might be to imagine.

Many metaphysicians have pondered the concept of nothing specifically in the context of the universe and our reason for existing. Gottfried Wilhelm Leibniz, a 17th–18th-century philosopher, questioned the very idea that anything exists at all. He declared that if there were things in the universe, espe-cially conscious things like humans and animals, then there have to be reasons for those things to exist.

This is what has caused us to come up with all sorts of reli-gions and frameworks for the universe and life's purpose—

because somethingness requires an explanation. How did it come to exist? And why does it exist in the particular way that it does?

Instead, he argued that nothingness is better, or at least simpler, since there does not need to be justification for its existence. This framework—that nothing is simple and something requires justification—would be taken up by another philosopher, Baruch Spinoza, who we will talk about later in this chapter.

☀ Frameworks of Somethingness

So, now that we've thoroughly explored nothingness, let's look at somethingness. It might seem like this is the simpler section, but just as Leibniz hypothesized, the existence of things requires a lot more explanation and raises a significant number of questions. There are two main questions to do with somethingness that we will explore in this section.

The first is a kind of metaphysics-epistemology crossover: "How do I know anything, even myself, exists?" This question explores how we perceive somethingness, taking some of the questions we explored in Chapter 1 about what constitutes knowledge further into the territory of what constitutes existence and matter.

The next question is "Why do things exist?" This question is the natural progression from Leibniz's proposition favoring the simpler nothingness hypothesis over somethingness since the latter seems to beg for justification. With these two questions, we will attempt to explore the counterpart of nothing.

1. Cogito, Ergo Sum

One of the most famous arguments for the existence of something was made by René Descartes, a French philosopher from the 17th century. Descartes began at the basest level of doubt, not taking any existence for granted, and thus he began with the framework that he couldn't assume anything to exist. He doubted the outside world, his senses, and even his own thoughts.

However, in doubting his own thoughts, he came to a realization: If he had the capacity to doubt his thoughts, then there had to be some sort of body to do the doubting. Thus, something must exist in order for the doubt to be able to occur. From this realization, he concluded, "I think, therefore I am," or in Latin, "Cogito, ergo sum." Descartes' declaration that he must at least have an existing mind in order to have conscious thoughts formed the basis for his definition of "something." For Descartes, the only "something" we can be completely sure of is our own thoughts, because even our senses deceive us.

2. Spinoza

The other major philosopher to address this question was Baruch Spinoza, another 17th-century philosopher. He was a science-based thinker who pondered the question of existence itself. However, unlike Descartes, who was mainly concerned with *whether* things existed, Spinoza was more concerned with *why* they existed. He was more in line with Leibniz in this way, asking why the universe is here and how we can justify its existence.

Do we ever discover who we are?

Spinoza came to the conclusion of inevitability. To him, the universe—or "something"—had to exist. He saw the universe as a complex machine of inevitably moving parts. This is a very similar theory to absolute determinism, which was discussed in Chapter 2. For Spinoza, the Big Bang—or whatever the inciting incident of the universe was—caused a chain reaction resulting in the exact conditions in which we live today. From here, we can see that Spinoza does not so much justify the existence of things so much as he shirks the need for a justification.

▶ The Construction of the Self

Most of us have had struggles with identity. You may be at a period in your life now (or perhaps in future) where you're more confident or comfortable with your identity than at other times. Often, people go through the strongest crisis of self when they are in their teens. According to Erik Erikson's theory of development, during ages 12–18, we go through a stage called "identity versus role confusion" in which we have to clearly define the type of person we want to be and secure the kind of place we want to have in the world.

This is why you often see teenagers trying on a variety of identities. Perhaps they've been studious intending to go to business school some day and now they're devoting all their time to oil painting and talking about moving to Europe, only to then discover an important social issue and start campaigning for a local charity. All of these stages are important for discovering who you are, but the real philosophical question is "Do we ever really discover who we are?" Or even better, "Is there even a self to discover?" We'd all like to think so, but many philosophers have questioned the basis for a sense of self or even for a distinction between the self and others. In this section, we will talk about some of the most interesting theories of self that have been developed by some of the world's greatest philosophers.

☀ John Locke's Argument: Consciousness as Self

Seventeenth-century philosopher John Locke developed a theory of self based on the contents of our consciousness. He essentially argued that people are themselves because they have a distinct rational brain and view of the world. We can think of this as a theory of subjectivity or a theory of filtering. Everyone has their own unique way of looking at the world, and no two people will react to a certain situation in the same way. Thus, your "self" is comprised of the subjective way your brain processes stimuli or emotion.

We can relate this to a certain philosophy of acting called "method acting," which was developed by Russian acting coach Konstantin Stanislavski in the late 19th century and further developed by American acting coach Lee Strasberg in the mid-20th century. This theory of acting aims to replicate another person's subjective responses, mimicking the way they would behave in a certain situation, so the actor's performance is based on this Lockean view—that we are who we are because of this unique filter of reality.

We can also see this through how artists view the world. The Impressionists, such as Claude Monet and Camille Pissarro, sought to create a subjective view of the world that can only be seen through their eyes. Thus, Monet's *Water Lilies* series does not depict the actual water lilies as such but instead depicts the water lilies as Monet saw them to be as viewed through his subjective filter. According to Locke, the Impressionists and the method actors were right, asserting their subjective perspectives as their true selves.

However, one potential challenge to this argument concerns people with DID, or Dissociative Identity Disorder (formerly referred to as Multiple Personality Disorder). Each identity has a distinct name, voice, personality, behaviorisms, and memories etc. Do we therefore deduce that an individual body can have multiple "selves", each with its own unique perspective on the world? Or is it that one self has multiple facets, all of whom look and behave as if they were independent selves?

Along similar lines, do people with BPD, or Borderline Personality Disorder (also known as Emotionally Unstable Personality Disorder) have no self because their sense of identity is so unstable? Their shifting sense of self can lead to failure to recognize who they *truly* are and what they want out of life.

☀ David Hume's Argument: Memories as Self

This is one we have already talked about, but here we are going to go into a little more detail. If you remember from our discussions of ethics as well as mortality, David Hume's "bundle theory" of the self purports that our self is not contained in a magical part of our minds influencing our every thought and feeling as Locke would have it. Instead, Hume believed that the self is simply a collection of our experiences. To Hume, everyone is born a blank slate. Potentially, we might experi-

Hume
Bundle Theory?

ence some things in the womb, but for the most part, we are born with no preconceived personality and are pushed toward one sensibility or another by the way in which we are raised.

Every moment, however small, contributes to the formation of our self. This is the reason it is known as the "bundle" theory: In this view, we continue to collect traits, memories, and influences throughout our lives that we can add to our bundle. The bundle theory also allows for a decent amount of change to happen throughout someone's life. If you collect enough alternative traits for your bundle, they will start to outweigh your former traits until you have completely changed. Basically, in Hume's view, you are what you experience.

The biggest wrench people throw in Hume's theory is amnesia. If a person lost all their memories, would they still be themselves? Well, according to a study reported on by *Psychology Today*, they would. In the study, doctors interviewed and assessed amnesia patients regarding their personalities while also asking these people's loved ones what they had been like before the injury.

In most cases, the two reports aligned very closely, suggesting that removing a person's memories does not have a strong impact on certain personality traits like extroversion, agreeableness, and so on. Thus, there must be more to the self than just memories (Fayard, 2021). However, this doesn't necessarily completely refute Hume. For example, the personality traits cultivated by experiences might not be completely conscious but instead more deeply internalized than amnesia reaches. Either way, studying how memory loss affects people can tell us a lot about the self.

☀ *Materiality as Self*

A third theory of the self concerns the physical body. According to this theory, you are yourself because you are made of the same materials from one moment to the next. Your physical body is what makes you the same person. This theory means that as long as you continue to have the same physical properties as you did before, then you are still alive. One major hole in this particular theory is that a dead person, or at least a very recently dead person, would be no different than a living person. But is a person who is dead the same as the person they were when they were alive? It's hard to say since many of the qualities we associate with the self would be gone. This is also true of how the body changes as we age. Even though you might have experienced continuity, your adult body might be completely unrecognizable from your child body, drawing into question whether you are the same person at all, at least from a materiality perspective. No matter what, there will be flaws with any theory of self.

☀ *The Ship of Theseus*

One of the most famous thought experiments in the field of selfhood and metaphysics is called the "ship of Theseus." This examines specifically the relationship between materiality and definitions when it comes to selfhood. The thought experiment is based on the ancient Greek hero Theseus, who was known to be a great seafarer. The ancient Greek philosopher

Plutarch came up with a thought experiment about one of Theseus' ships.

In the experiment, Theseus has a favorite ship, but it is getting old, and eventually, a board breaks on the deck. This board is quickly replaced, leaving the deck with one shiny new board among the old ones. Then, the next day, another board breaks, this time on the bow. This board is also replaced. And then every day after that, another board is broken and replaced, until every single board on the ship is replaced by new boards, with nothing of the old materials left. Is this the same ship as it was before? Even though Theseus has continued to sail on it and it looks exactly the same as the old ship, there is technically no physical trace of the old ship left, so is it the same ship? If Theseus had built a completely new identical ship and thrown away his old one, you would likely be more inclined to believe that these were two completely different ships. Let's review the two possible responses to this conundrum; either it's to be considered the same ship or it isn't.

1. It Is the Same Ship

If you believe that yes, it is the same ship, then you support the supremacy of definitions over materiality. You are probably a subscriber of the bundle theory, which prioritizes history over materiality. Since Theseus still thinks of his ship as the same one, calls it by the same name, and the ship still evokes the same memories in him, then it is the same ship.

One variation of the thought experiment that complicates this opinion is if the old boards were all salvaged from the garbage, repaired with glue, and put back together in the shape of the old ship. Now there are two ships, and it's as if he *did* simply create a new identical ship and cast off the old one. Would you say that there are still two ships? Which would you say holds claim to the real title of the ship of Theseus? The old one has the origins, but the new one has the continuation of the memories.

Another variation that throws a wrench in the "yes" answer is a scenario wherein Theseus' ship was replaced overnight by an exact replica without him knowing. He continues on as usual, treating his ship as he always has, but it is not the same ship in materiality. Would it be the same ship then? More people would probably say no to this than the original proposition. For those who believe that the idea of the ship is what makes it the same ship, there are still a lot of complications that can arise.

2. It's Not the Same Ship

If you believe that it is not the same ship, then you believe that the materiality of something makes it what it is. You don't believe that the ship is the same ship because its boards are different. In this case, you subscribe to the materiality theory of self, believing that things have to be materially the same in order to be thought of as actually the same.

A big criticism of this response to the thought experiment involves asking at which point did the ship stop being the same ship. Was it the replacement of the first board? The replacement of the last board? Or perhaps somewhere in between, maybe the halfway point? If you can't clearly pinpoint when the ship changed, then you can't truly identify the point at which the new ship emerged.

You might be tempted to say the halfway point is when it changed. However, a further complication would be a situation wherein half of the boards of the original ship were taken and reassembled into a new ship with new boards to make up the difference. You now have two identical ships, each made up of half of the original boards and half new boards. Which one has a claim to the title of the real ship if both of them have half of its original boards? As you can see, this situation makes it very difficult to categorize which is the real ship and which is the imitation.

What is perhaps most interesting about the thought experiment of the ship of Theseus is that it actually has very interesting implications for the materiality of human beings. Unbeknownst to the ancient Greeks, modern biologists have actually discovered that the human body is not unlike this famous ship. In fact, humans replace cells in our bodies all the time. Out of the 30 trillion cells in our bodies, we replace over 330 billion cells every single day, meaning that roughly every three months, you have a completely new body (Christiansen & Fischetti, 2021). Like the ship of Theseus, are you the same person? You still have the same memories, thoughts, and life situations, but you are, at least physically, a different person. When thinking about theories of the self, the ship of Theseus gives us a fascinating window into the world of selfhood and definitions.

▶ The Sorites Paradox

The final topic we will be discussing in metaphysics is the Sorites Paradox, a theory that attempts to define vague terms by degrees. It was first posited by the Greek philosopher Eubulides in the 4th century BCE. According to the Sorites Paradox, if something has an indeterminate parameter, then it's impossible to define what it actually is. The most famous example of this paradox is the problem of the heap. How many grains of wheat does it take to make a heap? Well, surely a thousand grains of wheat would qualify as a true heap. But if you start at the beginning and increase the amount by increments, things become hazier.

One grain of wheat certainly doesn't make a heap, nor do two or three, but at what point does it become a heap? If you say that three grains of wheat doesn't make a heap, but 25 grains do, we're left with a conundrum because that would mean that everything leading up to 25 isn't a heap, including 24 grains. Surely, the removal of one grain of wheat doesn't make the difference between something qualifying and not qualifying as a heap! No matter what number you pick, you're left with the paradox that the immediately preceding number(s) in your count can't be labeled a heap since you've defined the boundary at which one thing becomes another.

There are many variations of this, especially in idiomatic expressions such as "death by a thousand cuts" or "the straw that broke the camel's back." If you're thinking that this reminds you of the Ship of Theseus example, you're absolutely right. We pointed out that there is no clear point at which the old ship becomes a new ship since the boards are replaced incrementally, one by one.

From the perspective of metaphysics, this can draw into question many important terms we commonly use in society. For example, when do we become "old"? Is it when we reach a certain age? Even if you define an age that constitutes being old, such as 65, then is it on your 65th birthday that you become old? Are you not old at 11:59:59 pm on the day before your birthday and then instantly old at the stroke of midnight? And what about the difference in health between people, making some seem older than others, even though they are the same age? People in their late 20s and 30s sometimes start saying "I'm old!" when they start experiencing new aches and pains. They'll even say they're old by comparison to the new generation which has its own lingo and new technologies to play with that they didn't grow up with. By defining things in tiny increments, you create a paradox of definitions wherein the larger category (i.e., "heap" and "old") no longer exists.

5

SCIENCE

If we are ready to tolerate everything as understood, there is nothing
left to explain; while if we sourly refuse to take anything, even
tentatively, as clear, no explanation can be given.

—Nelson Goodman

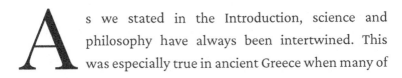s we stated in the Introduction, science and philosophy have always been intertwined. This was especially true in ancient Greece when many of

the most famous philosophers, such as Aristotle and Pythagoras, also practiced math and science. But these days, science and philosophy have somewhat split from one another in terms of fields of study. Instead, we tend to think of science as an intersection with philosophy, challenging or supporting philosophical theories.

For example, in the previous chapter, we talked about a scientific study of amnesia patients which then supported a philosophical idea. The intersection and collaboration between these two subjects are truly fascinating. There are so many things they have in common but also many ways in which they differ. Science can be used to back up philosophy, but it can also be used to challenge it and bring it back down to earth.

In this chapter, we will discuss the relationship between these two approaches in order to distinguish between them. First, we will look at the difference between the scientific method and the philosophical method and how those methodologies lead to a key difference between the two fields. Then, we will look at the mind-body debacle, debating the role of the soul versus biology. After that, we will talk about the idea of consciousness and what it really means to be conscious, according to both science and philosophy. And finally, we will look at how these two fields view the practice of learning. In these sections, you will gain a thorough understanding of the role of science within philosophy.

▶ Scientific Versus Philosophical Method

You probably learned about something called the "scientific method" in school. This is a specific methodology developed during the European Age of Enlightenment, around the 17th–18th centuries. It is not the only method for doing science, since science has been practiced in many places around the world for all of history, but this method has formed the modern Western foundation for scientific practice. This method consists of six phases which ensure that you have taken all steps necessary to carry out a reliable scientific experiment. The steps are

1. Ask a research question.
2. Conduct background research.
3. Construct a hypothesis or prediction about what you think the answer to your question will be.
4. Test your hypothesis with an experiment.
5. Draw a conclusion from your data analysis.
6. Write up your results.

Every step of this process is important to do properly in order for your scientific conclusions to be considered viable. This method has been used by countless researchers over the past couple of centuries and is responsible for a good portion of what we know in modern science today.

So, you know the scientific method, but is there a philosophical method? Well, sort of. Philosophy is much less regulated than science, thus there is no official methodology that all philoso-

Infinite questioning *Justified true Belief*

phers must use. However, one of the most common methodologies of philosophy, which we have been using throughout
this book, is infinite questioning. Most philosophical theories
start with some sort of framework of how the world is organized. Let's take justified true belief for example. To start, a
philosopher declares that JTB is the standard method for
measuring knowledge. The general method that follows for
other philosophers is to ask as many questions as possible and
come up with as many contradictory scenarios as possible in
order to poke holes in the original theory. Other philosophers
will come up with scenarios that might be outlandish and
extremely unlikely (as we saw with the Gettier problem), but
which nonetheless are theoretically possible and contradict
the framework. In the case of JTB, there could be some very
unlikely scenario wherein your justified true belief was still not
necessarily knowledge. Thus, we can see how philosophy
works more on the basis of cyclical building up and breaking
down of knowledge structures, always questioning any assertion and never letting an answer sit.

✸ Key Differences

There are a lot of important differences between the way scientists approach knowledge and the way philosophers do. One of
the key differences is that science is heading toward a definite
conclusion, while philosophy is not. Scientists might take a
long time to reach a conclusion, or even come to the wrong
conclusion, but nevertheless, the fifth and sixth steps of the
scientific method involve either confirming or disproving your
own hypothesis and thus need to be reached if you want to
complete the method. Philosophy, on the other hand, does not

Empiricism / Rationalism

necessitate an answer. Some philosophers might begin similarly to the scientific method—with a hypothesis—but there is no need for a definite conclusion. Many philosophical theories come to the conclusion that there is no conclusion, which is still a satisfying enough answer for philosophy and does not necessarily constitute a failure.

The other major difference between science and philosophy is that science is based on research out in the field, whereas philosophy is based on reason alone. You can't take a scientific theory seriously unless it has been tested on real-world things or people, whereas a philosopher need not leave their study, or even their mind. This difference in methodology actually has a name. The scientific method is known as empiricism, and the philosophical method is known as rationalism.

Empiricism is the idea that all knowledge must come from the outside world. According to empiricism, we can only learn through our senses, and anything we do know has come to us from the outside. This is why we see the scientific, or empiricist, method always doing research on real-world subjects since this methodology believes that practical research is the only way to obtain knowledge.

This may involve an experiment with a defined set of parameters and a control group for comparison of results. Ideally, the research would be conducted in a double-blind fashion, where fellow research assistants who are facilitating, or are actively engaging with participants of the experiment, do not know what the research is specifically aiming to prove or disprove. That allows the lead researcher(s) to rule out any conscious or unconscious biases on the part of the research assistants and any potential influence they may have on the outcome of the experiment.

Rationalism, on the other hand, believes that knowledge comes from the reasoning capabilities of the mind. If you are of sound mind and practice good logic, then you can come to conclusions about the outside world completely independently, without the need for research. Thus, you can see philosophers undergoing the scientific method in their own minds, coming up with thought experiments to illustrate their points and evaluating the outcome of those thought experiments based on their own capacity for logic. Although this isn't an objective methodology, it doesn't need to be. It doesn't matter who is doing the hypothesizing or what imaginative scenarios are being conjured up as long as the conclusion follows logically.

As mentioned earlier, sometimes there is no conclusion that we can logically assess. For example, is it possible that the wind can at some point blow fallen Autumn leaves into the shape of the word "hello" on the ground? Even with the prospect of infinite time, and the correlating notion that *everything* will theoretically happen in an infinite universe, we still can't deduce a concrete conclusion. We are therefore left pondering the question forever until, or unless, someone devises a sound logical argument that proves this is possible (or impossible). This actually may require some mathematical intervention to calculate probabilities. Something tells me, however, that mathematical formulas will be unable to prove that the possibility of this happening is zero.

From the dichotomy between empiricism and rationalism, we can divine some of the most pertinent ideological differences between science and philosophy.

☀ *Key Similarities*

Although we have contrasted the scientific and philosophical methods so far, they actually do have some important similarities. First of all, they both tend to start the same way—with a research question. You might even start a scientific study with the same research question as you would a philosophical study. For example: What is the purpose of dreams? This kind of question could spark a scientific experiment or a philosophical debate, yet they started in the same place.

Philosophy also uses experiments to illustrate points in the same way that the scientific method does. There are experimental qualities to philosophy, even if they are thought experiments. And in both cases, you write down and communicate your findings, the only difference being in whether those findings were external or internal. In essence, philosophy attempts to recreate the scientific method within the mind, using the faculties of reason to conduct experiments and test hypotheses. Therefore, even though they work in very different ways, philosophy and science really aren't so different.

▶ The Mind-Body Problem

Science has made a lot of headway when it comes to neuroscience, but philosophy still questions the role of the ephemeral mind in relation to the body. This question was particularly important to Descartes, the same thinker who came up with "cogito, ergo sum." For Descartes, the mind is disconnected from the brain, forming a difficult paradox wherein it can be difficult to see how the mind could possibly control the brain and vice versa. This is where science and philosophy really collide. From a scientific perspective, the brain, and other parts of the body, can be definitively measured. You can say that someone's body weighs a certain number of pounds, but you can't really say that a "mind" weighs any amount.

So, what is the mind? According to science, the mind is simply a function of the brain. All the cognitive functions of the brain are explained by neurons firing around. However, philosophers insist that there is something more to the mind than just the brain. There is an intangible quality to the human capacity for thought that can't be touched by physical reality. So what is the connection? How does the "mind" communicate with the body when it seems to be outside of the body? Descartes stated that this dichotomy, the materiality of the body and the immateriality of the mind, made it impossible to consider that they could interact with one another. Since the mind isn't made of anything, with no boundaries or materiality, what is tying it to the body?

This question represents the debate between two opposing ideologies: dualism and materialism. These two perspectives on the mind express this confusion about whether the mind is inherently connected to the physical brain or not. Dualists like Descartes believe that the mind and the body are split, that

Dualism vs *Materialism*

there is a physical brain and an immaterial mind that operate independently from one another.

Some cultures even acknowledge a third quality—the heart— as we see in the Japanese word *kokoro*, which is separate from the Japanese word for the physical heart in the body, *shinzou*. It defines an intangible network consisting of a person's ideas, thoughts, and feelings; this essence resides in the heart and can also be described as spirit. Could this be another immaterial part of the mind or soul that is separate from the body?

On the other hand, materialists believe that there is no separation between the mind and the body and that everything that happens in our "minds" is merely a function of the brain's chemistry. These thinkers don't believe that there is any evidence of another force outside the brain, and further, that there is no need for one. They argue that, because all the necessary and observed functions of the mind can be accurately described by scientific analysis of the brain, there is no need for this ephemeral force. Between these two arguments, we can see that the topic of the brain's materiality is an important part of the mind-body debate.

One of the main criticisms of dualism is that it fails to account for the functioning of the brain. If there is this ineffable mind, then what is the purpose of the brain? Why do we have a physical thinking machine in our heads if there is this immaterial force guiding the way we think? This is a key rebuttal of dualism in support of materialism. If the brain *can* think, then we have no reason to believe that it isn't thinking. When we use our "minds" during scientific experiments, scans can clearly see our brains firing, so what is the need to ascribe this activity to an outside source?

Another big point for materialism is that consciousness seems to stop after we die, or at least from observation. There has, to date, been no scientific evidence - at least according to those who dispute the validity of reincarnation - that someone has been conscious after they die, so there is no reason to believe that there is a mind outside of the physical brain. It seems that the physical brain has as much effect on one's thoughts—or one's ability to think at all—as it would if it were the only thing there was. Thus, from a scientific perspective, materialism is correct, and from a logical perspective, it seems much more likely.

▶ The Problem of Induction

How do we learn? What is it that helps us acquire new information? Well, there is education, where you attend school and memorize facts. You might learn about different periods of history, concepts in math, or strategies for writing an essay. But there is also a different kind of learning called induction. It describes the process of making inferences about things based on existing information. This is how we tend to learn out in the world. It's when you say, "I've experienced XY, so YX will probably be similar."

Our brains literally do this all the time. You do it when you try a new food, basing it on a similar food you like, or when you watch a new film by your favorite director, or even when you spend time with a new friend again because you liked their company the first time. It's also why you assume that people who come from hot places are more resistant to heat or that people who come from a country full of poets might have a natural sense of rhythm. It's generally how human beings characterize the world, making assumptions based on existing information. These induction patterns are sometimes known as frameworks or schemas, patterns through which we see the world.

However, induction and schemas can also lead us astray. These schemas that we use to categorize things might help us make quick judgments most of the time, but they can also take us in the wrong direction. It's why people tend to have prejudices toward groups of people about whom they have read bad news stories. It might even be the reason that people tend to be hesitant to start dating again after a bad breakup. When it comes to induction, it's all about associations, and when you create a negative association, you might be burning a bridge. In life, the brain tends to do this automatically. We naturally make these inductions every single day. But philosophers believe that there should be a more methodical approach to induction based on sounder reasoning.

So, what is the "problem of induction" according to philosophers? Well, the problem lies in a mismatch between the two premises. Let's take some of the examples we talked about before. If you like the film *Goodfellas* directed by Martin Scorsese (premise A), you might assume that you would also like the film *The Age of Innocence* because it was also directed by Martin Scorsese (premise B).

However, upon watching, you find the latter film very different and don't like it at all. So, what went wrong? Well, you based your second premise on an invisible middle premise. Premise B doesn't necessarily follow from premise A unless you believe that all films by the same director will be to one taste (premise C). However, upon reflection, you might realize that premise C isn't necessarily true, since many directors have a wide body of work. Thus, one of the main problems that can arise with induction is an implicit third (somewhat hidden) premise that might not necessarily be true. Let's look at another example.

Let's say you were cheated on by your partner and are now afraid to enter another relationship for fear of the same thing happening. Your train of logic would look like this: I couldn't trust the person I was with (premise A), therefore I won't be able to trust anyone else (premise B). This string of logic is ignoring implicit premise C, which is that people all act the same in a relationship. When we look at implicit premise C, we can see how the logic is actually based on a false equivalency, and when the lapse in logic is pointed out, it's clear how illogical the conclusion really was. Here we see the problem of induction. How can we come to conclusions about new things based on existing information about things we have experience with? Philosophy aims to regulate our logical sensibilities, forcing us to really follow the lengths of our own logic and examine whether there are any "implicit premise Cs" in the mix.

▶ What Is Time?

St. Augustine once famously said, "I know what [time] is if no one asks; but if anyone does, then I cannot explain it," illustrating that though we experience time on a daily basis, live inside it, and measure it, we don't really have a thorough understanding of it. Time is understood in a number of different ways, both by science and philosophy. Some of the world's most important scientists and philosophers, even poets and literary figures, have written extensively about the subject of time. There is a lot to understand about time and there are many pertinent questions about the ways in which time functions both in our minds and in reality.

For example, is time objective or subjective? Is there a grand experience of time that runs consistently or are we all on our own timelines? Is the past real? Is the future real? What is the present? And how can we express time to one another through different media? In this section, we will look at the philosophical, scientific, and even literary views on time to help us gain a sense of the way perception of time coincides with scientific representation.

☀ *The Philosophical View*

How do philosophers look at time? Well, there are many different views on the topic of time within philosophy. Time touches a lot of different branches of philosophy as well, such as metaphysics and free will versus determinism. Studying time as a philosopher helps you understand things like cause and effect, learning, and even life journeys.

The main issues expressed within the philosophy of time are the tension between subjectivity and objectivity as well as the roles of past, present, and future. In this section, we will look at these two major topics in the philosophy of time, shedding light on some of the main thinkers in these fields.

1. Time is Subjective

Is your time the same as my time? Have you ever come to work on Monday feeling like the weekend really flew by only to have a coworker talk about how long their weekend felt? Have you noticed that time seems to go faster as you have gotten older? These experiences are very common. Most people perceive time as passing at different speeds, depending on what they're doing—the adage "time flies when you're having fun"—and the perception of time speeding up as we age is a well-documented phenomenon.

The other reason we all have different perceptions of time is that our sense of time is strongly dependent on our memories. If you have a lot of memories of a certain event, it is likely to take up more space in your mind. Thus, we tend to assign more time value to more important periods in our lives. Your four years of college, which might have held a lot of change and memories, will likely seem like more time than 10 years in the same job. Thus, everyone not only feels time progressing differently, but we also perceive events in our lives as progressing at different rates from one another. But does this not fly in the face of the way we measure time?

2. Time is Objective

objective time

In the modern world, we have atomic clocks that keep track of every second with astonishing accuracy. We make plans based on this "objective" time, create train schedules, and track our lives. The invention of atomic clocks has pushed our sense of objective time even further.

As an aside, physicists Jun Ye and Hidetoshi Katori (who earned the 2022 Breakthrough Prize in Fundamental Physics) invented optical lattice clocks. Instead of our existing atomic clocks that lost one second every 100 million years, the new lattice clock astonishingly loses one second every 15 billion years (Daniel, 2021). That happens to be the approximate age of the universe so if this lattice clock theoretically existed at the moment of the Big Bang, in the present day on Earth, we'd only be one second behind in true time measurement!

How can we ultimately maintain a sense of objective time when we so clearly experience time subjectively? Does objective time truly exist or is it an artificial measurement humans created to facilitate the needs of society? This question has plagued philosophers for centuries and has been very important in the debate about time.

What parts of time are real? How can we define the relative reality of the past, present, and future? These are important questions that have produced three distinct perspectives on time. These different schools of thought represent ideas of what is real in terms of time. Here, we will examine Presentism, Eternalism, and Growing Block Theory.

1. Presentism

Only the present is 'Real'

Presentism is the perspective that only the present is real. The past and the future are not happening right now, so they cannot be said to be real. Because the future is undetermined and no one can say what is going to happen, it can't be said to be real. Real things must have substance, and because the future is insubstantial, it can't be said to be real. By the same logic, the past can't be said to be real either, because it only exists in memory. The only access we have to the past is either through the memories of people who experienced it or through evidence from which we can draw inferences.

One of the key thought experiments into the unreality of the past is the memory replacement theory. This thought experiment purports that everyone on earth could have just started to exist this second, with all the buildings, artifacts, and written accounts that illustrate the past being merely fabricated and all respective memories implanted into our heads. The thought experiment, though far-fetched, illustrates that we probably wouldn't know the difference between these two states of being and thus cannot say with certainty that it isn't happening. Thus, presentism denies the substance of the future and the reliability of the past, resulting in the conclusion that only the present is real.

2. Eternalism

Eternalism, on the other hand, states that the past, present, and future are all equally real. Eternalism constructs time as an imaginary line that extends out from the present both backward and forward, with each person's individual experience of time merely existing somewhere along that timeline. In this framework, time seems to be merely another spatial dimension on which people can exist at different points. This time-as-dimension theory will be explored further in this chapter. In essence, eternalism views all time as happening at the same time objectively, with individuals experiencing a subjective chunk of this eternal time. The present, in the eternalist view, does not exist objectively, only subjectively. It is nonetheless real, as stated.

3. Growing Block Theory

The growing block theory is somewhat of a middle ground between the two aforementioned theories. In the growing block theory, time is something that builds. Every present is like a building block constructing history. Let's imagine that every present moment is indicated with a wooden block that children play with. The next moment presents a separate wooden block that stacks on top of the former present moment, and so forth. The past is merely the sum total of present moments that have been calcified into an irreversible state.

☀ *The Literary View*

Literature is actually a great primary source for philosophy because it demonstrates how different people view certain subjective topics. Many creative authors have played with time. As we talked about in the last section, one view of time is as a narrative, so when fiction authors attempt to represent a narrative, it necessitates a view of time. Some novels take a very clear and linear view of time, describing events chronologically. But even these have to deal with the idea of pacing.

This relates back to the idea of subjective and objective time we discussed above. How do we represent the passage of time in different lengths? How do we create a realistic sense of time with only written words?

Some novels take a nonlinear perspective on time, either relying heavily on internal dialogue or representing events out of order. With internal dialogue, you are creating a space where the character is thinking, which is understood to be somewhat outside of time. In J.D. Salinger's *The Catcher in the Rye*, we can see how internal dialogue takes up time space, with a somewhat lengthy novel taking place over only the course of a day or so, and the rest of the space being taken up by the character's thoughts. Sometimes the changing of the order of time is actually meant to be confusing, such as in Ford Maddox Ford's *The Good Soldier*, which intentionally tells events out of order in order to play with the reader's sense of time. By playing with time in fiction, authors hijack our subjective sense of time and expand our sense of the elasticity of time.

In fiction, there is also the concept of "real time." This means that the work attempts to represent events at the pace that they would actually happen in real life. Hardly any novels take place in real time, both because of different reading speeds and the fact that internal monologue, which, as we have said, takes up a space outside of time, is so important in novels. One film that attempts to take place more or less in real time is Richard Linklater's *Before Sunset*, which follows two people walking around Paris, with the length of time that the characters are experiencing being almost the same as the actual length of the film.

This is an interesting experiment because it plays with our experience of subjective and objective time. Even if we are experiencing the same objective time as the characters, is our perception of time the same? A contrasting example would be Christopher Nolan's film *Memento*, which makes use of the jumbled quality of memory (or more accurately, short-term memory loss) to construct a disjointed story. It creates a subjective time, which is often actually experienced out of order within our own heads. These kinds of media help us to compare different perspectives on time.

One of the most interesting representations of time in literature—as well as film and television—is the idea of traveling through time. Science fiction stories from H.G. Wells's classic *The Time Machine* and the hit BBC series *Doctor Who* to Robert Zemeckis's film *Back to the Future* and recent raunchy comedy *Hot Tub Time Machine* all explore the concept of traveling through time. The fact that time travel is such a popular genre tells us a lot about our perception of time.

In many of these stories, we see time as a line along which we are traveling. With the help of magic, technology, or some other aid, we can jump back and forth on this line. Sometimes the characters can influence events, changing the future of the line, and sometimes the characters become part of events that had already happened in their timeline. But almost all of these representations treat time as objective, something that is neatly categorized by dates and numbers as opposed to something subjective or nonlinear. With these time travel stories, authors attempt to make sense of time and gain mastery over it, taming this extremely difficult topic with linear representation.

As an aside, one of the original time traveling heroes is Deathlok, a Marvel Comics character created in the mid-1970s. He returned from a post-apocalyptic future to influence the pending course of modern events. Since then, there have been numerous Marvel and DC comic heroes with similar abilities as well as drama series like "The Umbrella Academy". Featured on Netflix, it follows hero characters and their unique backgrounds and desires for influencing the future. There are also darker representations of time travel such as the Netflix series "Dark" and an abundance of other dramas available to us.

☀ *The Scientific View*

Science has its own perspective of time. The topic of time and time perception has been studied by many scientists. Throughout this section on time, we have referenced some of these scientific explorations of time and time perception, examining how they coincide with the philosophical view. Here, we will focus on the view of time through a scientific lens.

1. Subjective vs. Objective Time and Neuroscience

When it comes to perceptions of subjective and objective time, we have supporting evidence from the area of neuroscience. Professor Adrian Bejan explains that our neural processing speeds slow down as we age, meaning that there is less processing going on at a given time, and thus our brains feel like less is happening, and therefore time seems to move faster (Lazarus, 2020). This is usually a result of extensive experience with the same things, leading to less necessity for processing over time. If you do something every day, you don't need to process it as much, so the more experienced you are in life, the less you will need to process. Although this was not documented by the same study, it would be interesting to see if people who moved countries frequently experienced this same slowing-down effect or if their changing circumstances kept their processing levels up, causing them to experience a younger person's slower perception of time.

2. "The Present" and Neuroscience

There is also neurological evidence for the perception of "right now." According to some neuroscientists, we actually don't experience the present as it happens. Because of sensory delays, our brains actually don't process our perceptions until they have already happened. Thus, when you see your friend clap in front of you, the clap is happening a fraction of a second before you really perceive it. Thus, how can we say that the present is even real if we experience it out of synch? Thinking back to our philosophical theories of time (presentism, eternalism, and growing block theory), what does this neurological fact indicate? It seems that it might actually be creating a fourth theory of time, which could be called "past-ism." In pastism, only the past is real, the present being an ever-elusive state that we can never fully experience.

3. The Theory of Relativity

Only the past is real?

Perhaps the most revolutionary theory in all of scientific study of time was Albert Einstein's theory of relativity, published in different versions from 1904 onward. What this theory essentially posits is that time actually runs faster or slower depending on the speed at which you are moving. The closer to the speed of light you are traveling, the slower time will pass for you, relative to stationary people. The best way of illustrating this is through something called the "twin paradox."

In the twin paradox, one twin is sent out in a spaceship traveling close to the speed of light while the other twin remains on earth. Because of relativity, even if the space-traveling twin only goes up in space for a few hours, they will come back to earth years later. The earth-bound twin will have actually aged in that time, while the space-traveling twin will be the same age as they were when they left, give or take a few hours.

In this paradox, it's not just the perception of time that is different, but actual physical time, reflected in the relative ages of the participants. You could also illustrate this experiment with watches, which would have the same effect: the space-traveling watch would only count a few hours while the earth-bound watch would express long periods of time.

Einstein's theory of relativity obviously has huge implications for the subjectivity of time. From this theory, which has a strong basis in scientific reality, the concept of objective time has been completely obliterated. Now, there can't be said to be an official record of what day it is or how much time has passed, only what day it is on stationary Earth and how much time has passed according to the traveling speed of the ones recording.

If all of humanity got in a spaceship and traveled close to the speed of light, they might come back to a very different Earth. But if they kept their watches and calendars according to their own timeline, then how much time would have passed? On Earth, it might be hundreds or even thousands of years, but in space, it might have only been a few days. What if half of humanity did this while the other half remained on the ground? What would the date be then?

6

RELIGION

I do not know how to teach philosophy without becoming a disturber of established religion. –Baruch Spinoza

Philosophy has a long history of connection with religion. Many philosophers have also been religious leaders, such as St. Augustine and Nagarjuna. Many religions, particularly Christianity and Buddhism, have a long history of monasticism, which encourages deep philosophical thought and has inspired many writings throughout human history. Some people even consider religion itself to be a near branch of philosophy.

Contemplating God and the universe is part and parcel of religion, meaning that almost any religious text could also be a philosophical text. However, at the same time, many philosophers have been intensely critical of religion. Thinkers like Baruch Spinoza and Friedrich Nietzsche challenged the religious view of the world. In order to engage with theological philosophy properly, in their view, you have to truly entertain atheism as an option, otherwise, you are limiting your thinking.

In this chapter, we will discuss this topic, exploring how religion and philosophy intertwine. First, we will look at the fundamental question of whether or not God exists, examining different religious and atheist arguments. Then, we will discuss two categories of religions: monotheistic and polytheistic. And finally, we will look at different religions and how their depictions of deities influence their view of the universe's order. At the end of the chapter, your sense of religion's role in philosophy will be strengthened.

▶ Does God Exist?

The age-old question: Is there a God? Or, more specifically, is there a plan, an order, a creator for the universe? Please note: We'll be using the word "God" throughout this chapter, but if you prefer a different name or would rather refer to an overall universal omniscience instead, please substitute your preferred term or concept any time God is mentioned.

Most, if not all, cultures throughout history have come up with some sort of creation story for mankind, and many of them also refer to supernatural forces that influence the lives of humans. These forces can be God, multiple gods, higher-realm spirits, or any other force that reaches beyond physical reality. But the crux is that there is a spiritual plan for the universe, often with some kind of embedded moral code and potential punishment for wrongdoing.

The other stipulation is that there are almost never any actual physical signs of these forces, which is what makes them so mysterious and speculative. For this reason, almost all religions rely on faith in order for their supporters to believe in the existence of these supernatural beings. But because they exist according to faith alone, many people have questioned their existence, necessitating logical arguments one way or another. In this section, we will explore some of the most common philosophical arguments for and against the existence of God.

☀ The Case for God

Many philosophers over the course of history have been religious people and have thus come up with certain logical arguments for the existence of God. These arguments are as philosophical as they are theological, attempting to use the language and thinking skills of philosophy to make arguments in favor of the existence of God. Here, we will examine two such arguments: the causation theory and Pascal's wager.

1. Causation Theory

Back when we talked about the concept of nothingness, we discussed how Gottfried Wilhelm Leibniz argued that if something were to exist in the universe, there would have to be a reason for it. Well, this principle is actually very similar to the causation theory of God. Because the universe is something rather than nothing, there must be a cause for its existence. Thus, there must be some sort of divine being bringing the universe into existence. Otherwise, why would it exist at all?

This theory positions God as the answer to the creation, or causation, problem of the universe. It argues that there needs to be some kind of catalyst for the existence of the universe, which necessitates a God. *God causes everything*

2. Pascal's Wager *murder, disease, atom bombs*

The other major argument for God's existence is called Pascal's wager, which centers itself on the consequences for believing or not believing in God. The wager, posited by philosopher Blaise Pascal, is based on the valuing of rewards and punishments, which boils down to a version of Game Theory (which is based upon "players" in a situation having to make decisions based on various interdependent factors).

According to Pascal's framework, believing in God and not believing in God represent different risks. If you believe in God and God is real, you go to heaven (presumably). However, if you don't believe in God and God is real, you go to hell (again, presumably). Conversely, if God isn't real, then it doesn't matter what you believe, because everyone is going to the same place. Thus, believing in God gives you two possible outcomes, neutral or good, and not believing in God also gives you two options, neutral or bad.

Pascal's wager argues that it is a safer bet to believe in God since you risk nothing and have the chance for infinite rewards. Not believing in God is a much riskier choice since you stand to gain nothing, yet you also risk everything. This argument is not so much an argument as it is an incentive. Pascal wasn't trying to prove the existence of God, but rather that it's more favorable - in terms of potential benefit - to be a believer than a nonbeliever. Essentially, Pascal's wager argues that you should believe the argument from which you stand to gain the most.

Even if one were to dispute the notion of heaven and hell, the argument still holds because it's possible there will be some qualitative assessment of how you lived your life. Therefore, it probably behooves you to be respectful of God's existence, having believed in God all along, than to show disrespect for denying God's existence.

As an aside, basically every religion anthropomorphized God. Long ago, it was determined that God operates under the rules of humanity, making judgments, assigning either punishment or reward, having emotions such as anger, etc. However, it seems illogical that a human would be able to conceive of an omniscient power and its attributes since we ourselves aren't omniscient. We don't even know what it feels like to be a dolphin and use echolocation. It appears to us that they like to be social and engage in play, but do we know what they truly think? If we don't know how a dolphin thinks, how can we know what an omniscient being "thinks", if there is even any sort of thinking involved. To take it a step further, do God's "rules" apply only to Earth inhabitants or to every other potentially colonized planet as well? But I digress.

☀ *The Case Against God*

Just as many philosophers have argued against the existence of God as for it. There are many arguments for why God is illogical and doesn't make sense when held up to the philosophical method. Here, we will look at two arguments against the existence of God: the reverse causation theory and the problem of evil.

1. Reverse Causation Theory

The reverse causation theory is actually a response to the aforementioned causation theory. Since creationists argue that there must have been some sort of cause for the universe, they necessitate a creator. Their argument is that if there is something rather than nothing, then it would have required causation. The problem is that if God is something rather than nothing—and having the ability to create life in the universe certainly qualifies you as something—then, by the same logic, God would need to have been created as well. For this reason, the causation argument falls apart because if God needs a creator, then that creator needs a creator, and so on. This brings us back to the infinite regress we talked about back in Chapter 1—the "turtles all the way down" problem. The reverse causation theory essentially points out the fact that causation theory has a clear lapse in logic.

2. The Problem of Evil

The second major argument against the existence of God is the existence of evil, or at least the existence of innocent suffering in the world. God is supposed to be an all-loving figure, so how can there be suffering? Yes, there are tests and punishments, but there is no denying the reality that there are truly innocent children in this world who suffer and die. How is it compatible with a divine plan that there are innocents who experience suffer and die painful deaths? Many people find this to be their reason for not having faith—they simply cannot see how an all-loving deity could allow such things to happen.

This moral argument against the existence of God mostly applies to monotheistic religions like Christianity and Islam, since many polytheistic religions don't make the same claims about their deities. In the next section, we will talk about the difference between these two types of religions, the implications they have on the order of the universe, and the ways in which we experience morality.

▶ Polytheism Versus Monotheism

In the realm of world religions, there are two main frameworks: monotheistic and polytheistic. There are some exceptions, such as Buddhism, which doesn't have direct God figures per se, but for the most part, world religions are divided into these two categories. Monotheistic religions have only one God and generally consider that God to be perfect and all-knowing. Polytheistic religions, on the other hand, have multiple gods, ranging from a few to thousands. Usually, these religions consider their gods to be more fallible but still supernatural and extremely powerful. Polytheistic religions also often include a more open-ended pantheon with a wide array of gods that may or may not be included in different texts as well as different versions or manifestations of certain gods that represent them in different states.

These two versions of religion give us an interesting dichotomy in the world of religious philosophy. They allow us to see how gods and goddesses are represented in different ways and how that affects morality, world order, and the sense of a divine plan.

☀ *Characterizing God(s)*

One of the biggest contrasts between monotheism and polytheism is the characterization of the gods themselves. In general, God in monotheistic religions is represented as superhuman in both a physical and moral sense. These religions depict their God as being literally perfect and thus separate from humanity. Polytheistic religions, on the other hand, tend to have morally imperfect gods. They will engage in actions that people might see as morally reprehensible and even make self-admitted mistakes. These gods will be supernaturally powerful but more human in their desires and morally dubious actions. In this section, we will contrast these philosophies in more detail. These will be major generalizations that don't necessarily apply to all monotheistic or polytheistic religions, so for the sake of this section, we will just be contrasting Christianity with Greek mythology.

In Christian theology, which is monotheistic, God is perfect, supreme, and infallible. God, Jesus, and the Holy Spirit (or the Holy Trinity) represent the three components of perfection. God is a perfect moral arbiter and to suggest a mistake on the part of God or Jesus amounts to blasphemy. God, especially as represented in the New Testament, is also meant to conduct moral judgments of human beings based on this objective moral standard but never based on selfish vengeance or spite. From this perspective, even if God punishes people, it is always for their own or the greater good. This supports the idea of God's infinite love for humanity, represented as a sort of parental figure. This philosophy of God as all-powerful and all-loving is a way to ascribe a divine order to the universe, categorizing difficult events as the "mysterious" work of an ultimately benevolent God. It helps people to look toward the future and weather difficulties because there is a belief in an ultimate plan. From the monotheistic perspective, the world is orderly and neat.

In Greek theology, however, the gods are all very imperfect. There is not a morally infallible one among them. Even the nicest-seeming gods engage in wrath, revenge, lust, and all numbers of deadly sins. These gods are often punished by one another, such as Hera often taking revenge on her unfaithful husband Zeus. When the Greek gods punish humans, it's often for revenge as well, not necessarily as divine retribution, such as when Hera sabotages the Trojan army to take revenge on Paris for saying Aphrodite was more beautiful than her. This is not a morally bad offense, but since it offended a goddess, he was punished.

Here, we can see how polytheism takes a different view of the divine order of the universe, the gods being more like uncaring forces of nature than benevolent parents. These gods, which are often linked to divine forces such as the sea, lightning, or the sun and moon, express a more chaotic view of the world. Their mythologies help humans in a different way: to ascribe human rationale to these chaotic forces, assuming that Zeus must be angry when there is a bad storm or that Demeter must be depressed when a harvest fails. By taking these forces and turning them into human-like figures, the Greeks created a religious order out of chaos.

7

MORE INTERESTING QUESTIONS

Be a free thinker and don't accept everything you hear as truth. Be critical and evaluate what you believe in. –Aristotle

After reading this book, you might be wondering, *What do these questions have to do with everyday life? How can I apply all these high concepts to my actual existence?* Well, many of the thought experiments we've talked about have been very far-fetched, but that doesn't mean they don't have a practical application. In fact, many of these questions and thought experiments are merely academic ways of looking at very real problems in the world. The more you learn about the theoretical side, the more prepared you will be when you go back to the practical side. You might find that now that you have a basic background in philosophy, you are more prepared to go out into the world and consider those hard questions. Philosophy trains your brain to look for hard truths, not easy solutions, and in this way, it can turn you into a very valuable member of society, one who thinks critically and thoughtfully considers all sides of an issue.

In this chapter, we will go back through some of the key points we have discussed throughout the book, chapter by chapter, and apply some of these concepts to real-world discussions. The application of these concepts can vary among personal, interpersonal, judicial, political implications, and more.

▶ Epistemology

In Chapter 1, we discussed epistemology, which is the study of knowledge. In this chapter, we discussed what true knowledge really means and whether you can trust your senses. We asked key questions like "What is truth?", "Can we trust our senses?", and "What counts as proof?" As we explored these questions, we covered philosophers' viewpoints, but these questions also have practical implications.

Here, we will discuss how these questions apply to the studying or otherwise seeking out of factual data. As time progresses, the number of online sources for information continues to grow so this is particularly relevant today and will be even more so for the foreseeable future.

☀ *Understanding Sources*

Learning is a part of everyone's life, but where we learn from is as important as what we learn. Epistemology helps us question the sources of our information and really evaluate whether we are getting a clear picture or a biased one. Let's take Plato's Allegory of the Cave for example. When we learn, we often only get one perspective on a subject, unless we are looking at the real thing. Plato's Allegory of the Cave helps us understand the difference between a primary and a secondary source.

A primary source is a real document, so in the case of history, that would be letters from historical figures or objects from the past. These represent a real vision of history and correspond to the travelers in the allegory—the picture you are trying to see. Secondary sources are the reports people have made about a subject, such as a history textbook or a biography. They are filtered through someone else's mind and correspond to the shadows in the cave. This is not to say that secondary sources are bad—many are written by important scholars who add necessary context to the primary sources they work on— merely that they represent a picture of a picture, or the shadows on the wall.

You should try to use a combination of both types of sources so that you don't get stuck in the realm of shadows and take the opportunity to look at the travelers yourself. Also, beware of opinion, which may sound factual at times, but is solely based on one person's perspective and doesn't qualify as truth.

☀ *Debates and Logic*

If you have ever been part of a debate club, run for public office, or even just been in an argument, you have probably run into a fair number of logical fallacies. These can be very frustrating, especially when you don't understand them. In Chapter 1, we talked about some of the most common logical fallacies people use in arguments and explained what makes them unreliable. The next time you are debating with someone and find that they are using one of these fallacies - such as a circular argument - you will be able to point it out and explain where the problem resides. It can also help to make your own arguments more solid.

Being aware of logical fallacies and taking action to avoid them can help to strengthen your ideas and leave you less vulnerable to rebuttal. These epistemological tools can serve you well in the course of researching or presenting information. For the readers with children, however, how you manage your child's inquisitiveness is up to you; I have no philosophical guidance in that regard:

Child: Why can't we go to the park?
Parent: We can't get there because we need the car
Child: Why can't we use the car?
Parent: Because the car needs maintenance

Child: Why?

Parent: We didn't go for regular service like we should've

Child: Why?

Parent: Because we're busy at work

Child: Why?

Parent: %&#@!*

▶ Ethics

Moving on to Chapter 2, we discussed ethics. This chapter has perhaps the most obvious practical application since we do tend to make ethical decisions every day. No, you probably aren't going to have to drive any trolleys to avoid killing people tied to the tracks, but you might be in an ethical dilemma that requires hurting some people involved, even if just emotionally. In this section, we will present some more real-world examples of ethical dilemmas like the trolley problem.

☀ *Personal*

There are two main areas wherein ethics come up in real life—in personal and political areas. On the personal side, you have probably encountered many moral dilemmas. Maybe you were invited to two parties at the same time and had to choose between friends, or you had a loved one do something immoral and had to choose whether to forgive them. These dilemmas, no matter how small, can actually be helped by looking at different ethical frameworks laid out by philosophers.

Do you care more about the outcome or the intent? Are you intent on doing harm to the least amount of people or the least amount of harm to many people? How much does free will or determinism factor into your decision? Thinking about these bigger questions can help you make decisions with more clarity because you have those larger frameworks in mind.

☀ *Political*

We also tend to think about ethics when we are declaring our political opinions, either by voting or during verbal discussions. When we choose political affiliations, it is often for moral reasons. We think our political opinions represent what is best for people and are the least harmful. Those who advocate for policies that help the poor or disadvantaged believe that helping others is best and harm should be reduced at all costs, even if that means some people will get "handouts" or that it might be possible to "work the system" in some way.

And those who advocate for policies that punish the poor or disadvantaged are taking a more punitive perspective, believing that it helps people in the long run to enforce incentives to get a job or "pull themselves up by their bootstraps," believing that free opportunities cultivate laziness. This perspective can be presented in a way that you are doing something that appears unfavorable, but it's "for their own good" or "for the greater good".

These political perspectives are actually deeply rooted in long-running ethical schools of thought, such as free will versus determinism, equality of outcome versus equality of opportunity, and many more. Understanding the deeper place your political opinions come from can help you see them more clearly and understand what they are really advocating for at their root.

▶ Mortality

We all will die, but most importantly, we all will also have to deal with death at least a few times throughout our lives before our own. In Chapter 3, we looked at some of the world's views on death as well as certain philosophical perspectives. The way we view death or practice rituals surrounding death can greatly influence our perspective on it and methods of processing grief. Learning about different cultural practices and evaluating how you really feel about the afterlife can certainly help you come to terms with death and grief more deeply than you would have otherwise. Here, we will examine some of the ways a more philosophical understanding of death can look in the real world.

☀ *Grief*

When someone dies, there is going to be confusion. Even if you have firm beliefs about the afterlife, there is still an element of mystery to the place people go after they die. You might find it hard to really have closure if you are unsure about the afterlife, not knowing whether your loved one is still around or whether their consciousness has ended. Learning about different principles of the afterlife can help you ask these questions head-on and perhaps gain a more nuanced perspective of the afterlife and the processing of death.

It may also impact how you emotionally process the death of a loved one. You may feel that a certain length of time is required for you to formally grieve the loss or you may have a revelation that your loved one wouldn't want you to suffer each day and would want you to celebrate the happy times and the memories of the life that was.

☀ *Accepting Your Own Death*

Depending on the circumstances and/or age, you will probably start to confront your own death at some point. Some of us have social circles in which someone who was diagnosed with cancer as a teenager, or an otherwise healthy 30-year old suddenly suffered a heart attack. Then there is always the possibility of an accident. Not to be terribly morbid, but your tomorrow is never guaranteed so we shouldn't assume we'll be here tomorrow.

That being said, the vast majority of us assume we'll be alive for a very long time and death is somewhere off in the distant future. This isn't something you should start obsessing over, but it may not be a bad idea to get the "organ donor" designation on your license if you plan to help others in the event of your unexpected passing. Drop hints with your loved ones regarding your passing. My significant other has known for years that I'd like my ashes to be used in the formation of an artificial reef (ball) to support the restoration of marine life to coastal Florida (see eternalreefs.com for more information). Others donate their bodies to scientific research. To each his/her own.

Those who reach old age, or perhaps those who are diagnosed with a terminal illness, will in a sense be forced to contemplate their mortality. Again, whether or not you have secure opinions about the afterlife, this concept can still carry a lot of mystery and confusion for you. You might struggle to accept that you really are going to die, or rather where you are going to go after you die. Coming to a clear and deliberate decision about what you believe can make dying seem a little less mysterious or daunting and can help you cross that threshold with more peace.

▶ Metaphysics

Metaphysics, which we discussed in Chapter 4, is a little less clearly applicable to real life but nonetheless still has some interesting things to say when it comes to the real world. We can gain a more nuanced understanding of selfhood and the world around us. Asking questions about the nature of our own existence is an important exercise that can broaden our perspective and help us construct an identity. Here, we will look at some scenarios that involve a metaphysical understanding of the world.

☀ *Identity Building*

George Bernand Shaw said that "life isn't about finding yourself. Life is about creating yourself". If this is true, then knowing a fair amount about how humans construct identity can do wonders for your sense of self. Thinking back to some of our selfhood frameworks from Chapter 4 can help you consider the foundations upon which you've constructed your own identity over the years. Do you believe in a self-assertion narrative in which your unique perspective on the world creates your sense of self, or do you believe in the bundle theory, where everything that happens to you works to create your personality?

Both of these differing perspectives can have a major effect on the way you perceive yourself. If you take the former route, you will likely be more self-defining and independent, not letting the people around you or where you come from affect the person you are. If you subscribe to the latter school of thought, then you likely will have a strong fidelity to your family and hometown, acknowledging their role in your upbringing and creation of self. In these senses, your framework creates yourself as much as any other force and can help you gain a deeper understanding of who you are and how you think about yourself.

☀ *Finding Your Place in the World*

Metaphysics is also concerned with how human beings relate to one another and the world at large. Martin Luther King, Jr. once said "Life's most persistent and urgent question is, 'What are you doing for others'?". Understanding your own perspective on existence and the ways people function can help you create a grander narrative about your life and the way the world works. Concepts like the sorites paradox can help you learn to define things in the world more clearly, questioning how existing definitions work. When you educate yourself on other perspectives, you make yourself into a more well-rounded person who can contribute more to society.

▶ Science

Science is absolutely practical, but the philosophical study of how science is done is equally practical. Understanding the scientific method and its relationship to the philosophical method can be a great way of developing your methodology, especially if you are a scientist yourself. Science might seem infallible, but there are many ways in which parts of the scientific method can be done incorrectly, resulting in invalid experiments or biased results. Having a thorough philosophical background on the relationship between science and philosophy can help you really dig deep into the important questions at the base of science itself. Here, we will discuss some of those important questions in a more practical context.

☀ *Methods of Science*

Since we explored the scientific method in Chapter 5, including its similarities to the philosophical method as well as its differences, you now have a more thorough sense of the way in which science is done. If you engage in scientific work, you can see how it is meant to be done properly. Thought experiments in philosophy can help you understand how the mind processes logic and possibly even help you construct better experiments. Using the philosophical method of thought experiments can thus help you save time as a scientist, helping you to run scenarios through the lens of logic before you start to actually investigate them in the real world. You might actually end up saving yourself some effort.

☀ *Evaluating Science and Scientific Reporting*

If you are not a scientist, you likely still encounter science through articles or other news sources. We encounter many scientific studies in life that help us make decisions about nutrition, environmental responsibility, and other things. When reading a scientific study, or even a report about a scientific study, it's very important to pay attention to those last few steps of the scientific method—conclusion and presentation. When you look at these closely, you can see where someone might be reporting a biased version of the experiment's findings or coming up with conclusions that don't necessarily follow the evidence. As an informed citizen, it is imperative that you use your critical thinking skills from both philosophy and science to evaluate how the facts are being reported and whether you think they are being reported honestly. This will help you ascertain the viability of studies and become more critical and honest in how you see the world.

▶ Religion

A contentious topic at the best of times, religion has a strong relationship to philosophy. Religious debates about the existence of God have gone on for millennia, often being central to famous works of art or literature and even the catalyst for major wars. In Chapter 6, we talked all about different perspectives on religion, presenting arguments for and against the existence of God. These debates might seem purely spiritual, but the reality is that religion is and always has been deeply political, so these debates and debate methods are as relevant as ever. Here, we will look at some of these pragmatic implications for debates around religion.

☀ *Faith*

We all have faith in something, whether it is God, other people, artistic pursuits, or something else entirely. Almost everyone has a pursuit or a group or a belief that they feel is outside themselves and contributes to society at large. This belief is usually based on faith that something is inherently good or healing, such as community, music, art, or organized religion. No matter what you have faith in, that faith likely has some kind of ethical principles, even if they are as simple as committing to artistic integrity or being kind to one another. In both cases, understanding the general ethical principles of world religions can help you understand how your own faith works in practice and keep you honest about your own beliefs.

☀ *Politics and History*

Religion plays a major role in many societies around the world, being tied up with political movements, artistic movements, and even wars. From a judicial standpoint, up until just over five decades ago, witnesses in court proceedings were required to swear an oath on the Bible. Although this pre-requisite was phased out, there are times at which we still see religion at play. For example, when Ketanji Brown Jackson was sworn in as a US Supreme Court Justice, she had her left hand on two bibles as she did so. This happened in mid-2022, relatively recently as of the writing of this book.

If you struggle to understand the underpinnings of religion, or even how different religions see morality and responsibility, then much of human history and current events will be obscure to you. Investigating these difficult questions can help shed light on some of life's most difficult problems and make you a more tolerant person toward groups or movements that you might have otherwise been suspicious of. Understanding religion as a concept, especially from a philosophical point of view, breeds tolerance and understanding.

CONCLUSION

Philosophy may have seemed like a gargantuan, impenetrable topic previously, but now it is hopefully a little clearer. Throughout this book, you likely encountered questions that you have contemplated before, perhaps during conversations with friends or even alone late at night. What is important about philosophy is both realizing that many other people have pondered these very same questions and that they have come up with interesting answers. You can learn from these answers and add them to your own array of philosophical ideas. But learning about philosophy isn't just about collecting an array of theories and memorizing them. It is not like history or science class where the important things are in the facts. No, philosophy is a way of thinking more than it is a collection of theories.

You might not have learned about every single philosopher or philosophical theory in this book, but what you have learned is a philosophical way of thinking. It's the "give a man a fish and he will eat for a day, but teach a man to fish and he will eat for a lifetime" principle. If you learn a few philosophical theories, you will have a more nuanced understanding of those specific topics, but if you learn the philosophical way of thinking, then you will be able to ascribe philosophical ideas of your own to almost any situation.

So, what is this philosophical way of thinking that we have been practicing throughout the book? Well, it is one based on logic, reason, and endless questioning. Philosophers thrive on questions and will always pick apart answers when they arise. To a philosopher, anything is fair game for questioning. However, it is not blind questioning but rather very targeted. Philosophy questions because it aims to get to the root of a concept. It aims to discover what is underneath the everyday beliefs we have.

Your politics, sense of identity, and faith all have deeper roots that can be examined more closely if you take a philosophical view of things. You can challenge the status quo, discover new things about yourself, and become more tolerant of other people if you take this deeper understanding of the world to heart. Throughout this book, we have given many examples of how philosophers achieve this kind of reasoning, so you should now be able to come up with your own thought experiments, pick apart others, and come up with more complex ways of describing the world. In other words, you are on your way to expanding your mind and achieving a deeper understanding of everything that is.

If you are interested in learning more about philosophy, a great place to start is by researching one of the philosophers mentioned in this book. A number have been mentioned, and only one a couple ideas or theories were provided for each. Many of these philosophers have much more to offer, and you'll quickly find no shortage of other philosophers who gave counter-arguments or rebuttals of prior ideas. Consider further reading in order to gain a more in-depth understanding of any of the topics that were of interest to you.

If you enjoyed this book, I'd be grateful if you would leave a review on Amazon. There are other people like you who are searching for a book like this and your review will elevate its visibility to those seekers.

One final remark: Think deeply, question everything, and keep your mind open to new possibilities!

APPENDIX A - PHILOSOPHERS

Aristotle - Greek philosopher (384 BCE - 322 BCE)

Student of Plato

- Life as a Biological Property

Proposed that life is defined by a number of biological functions or properties such as nutrition, reproduction, ability to sense and move independently.

—— See Chapter 3 - Mortality

- Life as Vitalism

Proposed there's a substance at our core that's responsible for the creation and sustenance of life. This life force is independent from our physical bodies and is often referred to as a soul. We can relate this theory of life to the concepts of the soul, chakras, or chi, which also identify a kind of core life force within us.

— See Chapter 3 - Mortality

Bentham, Jeremy - English philosopher (1748 - 1832)

Together with John Stuart Mill, he proposed a secular system of ethics, meaning one that is independent of religious themes, called Utilitarianism. Utilitarianism proposed the existence of a morality that is good for its own sake.

Jeremy was also a proponent of Hedonism, where happiness is achieved via the experience of pleasure (which may or may not be achieved morally).

— See Chapter 2 - Ethics and Morality

Chisholm, Roderick - American philosopher (1916-1999)

- The Problem of the Criterion

Proposed that definitions of some common terms aren't exact, and thus we cannot truly confirm that something is what we say it is. Everyone "knows" what a pet is, but what are the specific characteristics of a pet? If it's an animal in your home, would the occasional spider making a web on your ceiling also qualify as a pet?

— See Chapter 1 - Knowledge

Descartes, René - French philosopher (1596-1650)

Proposed that we can't assume anything exists, except for our own thoughts. Since we use thought to question the nature of existence, Descartes came to the conclusion of "I think, therefore I am" and that is the only thing he can be sure of.

— See Chapter 4 - Metaphysics

Proposed the mind isn't connected to the brain. The dichotomy between the materiality of the brain and the immateriality of the mind makes it impossible to consider that they could interact with one another.

— See Chapter 5 - Science

Eubulides - Greek philosopher (4th century BCE)

- *The Sorites Paradox*

Discussed the vagueness of certain terms, and how it's impossible to define the point at which one thing becomes another when measured in increments. If you start with one grain of wheat and start adding to it, at what point does it qualify as a "heap"? One or two grains of wheat don't qualify as a heap. If we say 25 grains of wheat comprise a heap, does that mean that 24 grains does not? Where is the defining moment?

— See Chapter 4 - Metaphysics

Foot, Philippa - English philosopher (1920 - 2010)

- *The Trolley Problem*

This thought experiment investigates the boundaries of harm reduction ideologies like utilitarianism. The hypothetical situation - and variations thereof - forces an individual to make a choice by identifying the best course of action (or inaction).

— See Chapter 2 - Ethics and Morality

Gettier, Edmund - American philosopher (1927 - 2021)

- The Gettier Problem

Proposed that Justified True Belief is too vague of a framework for qualifying knowledge. The parameters of "knowing" whether a friend of yours would like a certain book aren't necessarily valid, but you would never know the parameters upon which you base your "knowledge" were invalid.

— See Chapter 1 - Knowledge

Hume, David - Scottish philosopher (1711 - 1776)

- Bundle Theory

Proposed that the concept of "self" is defined as a collection of our personal experiences in life. Individuals are born as blank slates and form their identity, including traits and personality, throughout their life. This is a malleable definition of self because you can change over time based on your experiences.

— See Chapter 4 - Metaphysics

Leibniz, Gottfried Wilhelm - German philosopher (1646 - 1716)

APPENDIX A - PHILOSOPHERS

Proposed that nothing is simple and something requires justification. The existence of something requires justification for its existence, sort of like a burden of proof.

— See Chapter 4 - Metaphysics

Locke, John - English philosopher (1632 - 1704)

Proposed that the concept of "self" is defined by the content of our own unique and subjective consciousness. This includes the way in which we individually process our environment, react to stimuli, etc.

— See Chapter 4 - Metaphysics

Mill, John Stuart - English philosopher (1806 - 1873)

Together with Jeremy Bentham, he proposed a secular system of ethics, meaning one that is independent of religious themes, called Utilitarianism. Utilitarianism proposed the existence of a morality that is good for its own sake.

John was also a proponent of Hedonism, where happiness is achieved via the experience of pleasure (which may or may not be achieved morally).

— See Chapter 2 - Ethics and Morality

Molyneux, William - Irish writer (1656 - 1698)

- Molyneux's Question

Questioned whether a person born blind - who was given several shaped blocks (cubes, spheres, etc) to identify using tactile sensation through the hands - would be able to identify the same shapes if they were suddenly given the ability to see. They wouldn't be allowed to use their tactile senses as before. Essentially, are the forms you perceived with one sense recognizable via a different sense?

— See Chapter 1 - Knowledge

Nagel, Thomas - American philosopher (1937 -)

- Control Principle

Proposed that people can't be held responsible for things beyond their control. People shouldn't be judged by intent or outcome, but rather by the knowable and controllable factors at the time.

— See Chapter 2 - Ethics and Morality

Nietzsche, Friedrich - German philosopher (1844 - 1900)

Challenged the religious view of the world. In order to engage with theological philosophy properly, in their view, you have to truly entertain atheism as an option, otherwise, you are limiting your thinking.

— See Chapter 6 - Religion

Pascal, Blaise - French philosopher (1623 - 1662)

- Pascal's Wager

Proposed that it's a safer bet to believe in God than not. If you believe in God, a real entity, you'll go to Heaven as opposed to going to Hell for disbelief. If God isn't real, it doesn't matter what you believe since there's no consequence. Not believing in God is riskier because if God exists, there will be negative consequences for your disbelief (versus believing, which leads to infinite reward). The core of the argument is to take the side from which you stand to gain the most.

— See Chapter 6 - Religion

Plato - Greek philosopher (428/427 BCE - 348/347 BCE)

Student of Socrates

- Allegory of the Cave

This thought experiment portrays that we cannot believe that something is true based on our senses alone. Our view of an object, for example, may not give us a full and true representation of the real object. The truth of an object is beyond our perception and exists in the world of "ideal" type forms.

— See Chapter 1 - Knowledge

- Justified True Belief

This includes having a belief that is both true and true for a good reason. To be able to conclude that you have knowledge of something, you must *believe* that it is true and also you must have good reason for thinking that it is true.

— See Chapter 1 - Knowledge

Plutarch - Greek philosopher (46 - 119 AD)

- Ship of Theseus

Proposed this thought experiment based on the Ancient Greek hero Theseus and his ship which is deteriorating and requires the replacement of deck boards, one at a time. The question concerns the identity of the ship - at what point is it no longer the same ship? Or does it maintain its identity throughout the replacement of all ship boards?

— See Chapter 4 - Metaphysics

Rosenberg, Jay - American philosopher (1942 - 2008)

Life is defined by biography, accumulation of experiences. Therefore, is life merely a sequence of events, bundled together only by the fact that the same person has experienced them? This perspective is related to David Hume's bundle theory of the self.

— Chapter 3 - Mortality

Sartre, Jean-Paul - French philosopher (1905 - 1980)

Proposed that human beings have complete control over their thoughts and actions and should be held responsible for every action they take. In this view (radical free will), there's no other factor influencing a person's action

— See Chapter 2 - Ethics and Morality

Spinoza, Baruch - Dutch philosopher (1632 - 1677)

Proposed that it's inevitable for something to exist (versus nothing). The Universe has to exist because it's a complex operation of cause and effects that result in the world we live in today. He doesn't feel justification for the existence of something is necessary.

— See Chapter 4 - Metaphysics

APPENDIX B - DEFINITIONS

Biological Reductionism

This position dictates that all activities of the mind are purely systems of biology and chemistry. What we call the soul is simply the complex work of brain cells and no consciousness survives beyond death.

— See Chapter 3 - Mortality

Causation Theory

This theory posits that because the universe is something rather than nothing, there must be a cause for its existence. Thus, there must be some sort of divine being that was the catalyst for creating the universe, thereby causing it to exist.

— See Chapter 6 - Religion

Circumstantial Determinism

Focuses on the limitations of free will based on circumstances. A person believes it's morally wrong to steal food, but makes the decision to do so based on the unfortunate alternative of starvation. People are less accountable when factors beyond their control determine the action taken.

— See Chapter 2 - Ethics and Morality

Eternalism

This is a perspective on time that declares that past, present, and future are all real. The past is as real as the future and the present. Time is viewed as a dimension and our subjective experience of time can exist at any point, along any line, within that dimension. All time is happening concurrently (and objectively).

— See Chapter 5 - Science

Growing Block Theory

This is a perspective on time that takes a middle-of-the-road approach landing somewhere between presentism and eternalism. Time is something that builds like a construction project that happens by stacking many presents on top of each other to create a history, which is irreversible.

— See Chapter 5 - Science

Humanism

Ideology that's focused on human connection and community where the meaning of life is humanity-based, rather than spiritual or religious. All of humanity is deemed equal and superior, above other living beings, and connecting with each another is the ultimate expression of life's meaning.

— See Chapter 3 - Mortality

Internal Determinism

Focuses on limitations of free will based on the mind, including mental illness, trauma, etc. Someone with a phobia of leaving their home has the physical ability to do so but is prevented from doing so by their fear. Factors within someone's mind can have an impact on their actions, rendering them less responsible.

— See Chapter 2 - Ethics and Morality

Limited Free Will

Human beings are responsible for almost all of their actions, barring extreme acts of chance. Generally speaking, we have control over our fate.

— See Chapter 2 - Ethics and Morality

Moral Luck

Evaluates the role that intention and outcome play in defining a person's responsibility for an action or decision. The "luck" aspect comes into play when the intention and outcome are inconsistent with each other.

— See Chapter 2 - Ethics and Morality

Nihilism

This position simply states that life has no meaning. A similar term - skepticism - is more broadly utilized but isn't quite the same as nihilism. Skeptics believe there's no meaning in the world other than the meanings we humans assign to things. This denies the potential existence of an absolute truth for us to discover.

— See Chapter 3 - Mortality

Posthumanism

This movement is a critical response to humanism. Posthumanism recognizes the importance that plants and animals play and that we don't have a free pass to exploit the planet's resources on account of our perceived superiority. We have ethical responsibility not just for ourselves, but for the broader picture of all that exists on our planet.

— See Chapter 3 - Mortality

Presentism

This is a perspective on time that declares that only the present is real. The past and the future are not currently happening, so they cannot be said to be real. The future is undetermined and the past only exists in memory so neither can be considered real. Thus, presentism denies the substance of the future and the reliability of the past, constructing the present as the only real thing.

— See Chapter 5 - Science

Radical Determinism

This is the opposite of radical free will. Everything in existence is predetermined and there's no free will. From this angle, if you gave a supercomputer the details of everything that's happened in the past, it'd be able to "predict" the future on the premise of cause and effect. This extreme view means no one is responsible for anything.

— See Chapter 2 - Ethics and Morality

Radical Freedom

Human beings have complete control over their thoughts and actions and therefore must be held responsible for every action they take. There are no "mystical" forces acting upon or influencing our decisions. We are also accountable for our actions in the broader sense of how our actions impact the rest of humanity.

— See Chapter 2 - Ethics and Morality

Reverse Causation Theory

The reverse causation theory is a critical response to the Causation Theory. Since creationists argue that something must have caused the universe to exist, then by that same logic, something must have caused the divine being (who created the universe) to exist. If that's the case, then what created the creator of the divine being who brought the universe into existence? We can regress infinitely using this logic so causation theory has a clear lapse in logic.

— See Chapter 6 - Religion

Transhumanism

This movement is a response to posthumanism. Transhumanism focuses on exceeding our body's current limitations to become "post-human". Technologies such as artificial intelligence, genetic engineering, and nanotechnologies pave the way for redefining what it means to be human. Our life experience can be enhanced both physically and mentally. We may at some point discover how to slow or stop the aging process and live fuller lives.

— See Chapter 3 - Mortality

Utilitarianism

Good and bad are defined through inherent morality, independent of judgment or reward. It's comprised of three aspects:

- 1. Happiness and pleasure are valued above all else.
- 2. Happiness and pleasure are equated with good, meaning that actions that promote these two things are considered good.
- 3. All people's happiness counts equally.

— See Chapter 2 - Ethics and Morality

BIBLIOGRAPHY

8 Daily Life Examples Of Axioms. (n.d.). StudiousGuy. https://studious-guy.com/daily-life-examples-axioms/

10 variations of the trolley problem to explain the difference between climate action and inaction. (n.d.). LinkedIn. https://www.linkedin.com/pulse/10-varia-tions-trolley-problem-explain-difference-young-jin-choi-frsa

202 philosophical questions—A huge list of thought provoking questions. (2017). Conversation Starters World. https://conversationstartersworld.com/philo-sophical-questions/

About Teleological Behaviorism - Scientific Figure on ResearchGate. Available from: https://www.researchgate.net/figure/Platos-allegory-of-the-cave-Drawing-by-Markus-Maurer-Licensed-under-the-Creative_fig1_311947836

Agnosticism about God's existence. (2022, January 6). 1000-Word Philosophy: An Introductory Anthology. https://1000wordphilosophy.com/2022/01/05/ag-nosticism-about-gods-existence/

Agrippa's trilemma—Pyrrhonist tranquility. (2012, August 12). Tim Neal: Philo-sophical Writings. https://timjohnneal.wordpress.com/2012/08/12/agrippas-trilemma-pyrrhonist-tranquility/

Agrippa's trilemma and the meaning of life. (2022, February 20). The HR Philoso-pher. https://hrphilosopher.com/2022/02/20/agrippas-trilemma-and-the-meaning-of-life/

Arguments for God. (n.d.). Creation. https://creation.com/arguments-for-god

Aristotle quote. (n.d.). A-Z Quotes. https://www.azquotes.com/quote/1397505

Asklepios: Greek god of medicine & doctors. (2017). Theoi. https://www.theoi.-com/Ouranios/Asklepios.html

The badness of death. (2014, May 1). 1000-Word Philosophy: An Introductory Anthology. https://1000wordphilosophy.com/2014/05/01/the-badness-of-death/

Baruch Spinoza quote. (n.d.). A-Z Quotes. https://www.azquotes.com/quote/279826

Because God says so: On divine command theory. (2014, March 31). 1000-Word Philosophy: An Introductory Anthology. https://1000wordphilosophy.-com/2014/03/31/because-god-says-so/

Bolter, J. D. (2016). Posthumanism. *The International Encyclopedia of Communica-*

tion Theory and Philosophy, 1–8. https://doi.org/10.1002/9781118766804.wbiect220

Borderline Personality Disorder (BPD). (n.d.). HelpGuide.org. https://www.helpguide.org/articles/mental-disorders/borderline-personality-disorder.htm

Britannica, The Editors of Encyclopaedia. "Pascal's wager". Encyclopedia Britannica, 11 Oct. 2022, https://www.britannica.com/topic/Pascals-wager

Bundle theory of mind. (n.d.). Routledge Encyclopedia of Philosophy. https://www.rep.routledge.com/articles/thematic/mind-bundle-theory-of/v-1#:~:text=This%20theory%20owes%20its%20name

Camilleri, A. (n.d.). *Existentialism, radical freedom, and anguish*. PhilosophyMT. https://philosophymt.com/sartre-radical-freedom-and-anguish/

Children Who Report Memories of Previous Lives. (n.d.). University of Virginia School of Medicine Division of Perceptual Studies. https://med.virginia.edu/perceptual-studies/our-research/children-who-report-memories-of-previous-lives/

Christiansen, J., & Fischetti, M. (2021). Our bodies replace billions of cells every day. *Scientific American*. https://doi.org/10.1038/scientificamerican0421-76

Cogito, ergo sum. (2019). Encyclopædia Britannica. https://www.britannica.com/topic/cogito-ergo-sum

Consciousness. (n.d.). Internet Encyclopedia of Philosophy. https://iep.utm.edu/consciousness/

Craig, H. (2019, January 21). *The philosophy of happiness in life (+ Aristotle's view)*. Positive Psychology. https://positivepsychology.com/philosophy-of-happiness/

Coulter I, Snider P, Neil A. Vitalism-A Worldview Revisited: A Critique Of Vitalism And Its Implications For Integrative Medicine. Integr Med (Encinitas). 2019 Jun;18(3):60-73. PMID: 32549817; PMCID: PMC7217401.

D'Olimpio, L. (2019, February 22). *The trolley dilemma: Would you kill one person to save five?* The Conversation. https://theconversation.com/the-trolley-dilemma-would-you-kill-one-person-to-save-five-57111

Daniel, H. (2021, September 14). *The world's most accurate clock*. Labroots. https://www.labroots.com/trending/chemistry-and-physics/21278/world-s-accurate-clock-2

David Hume quote. (n.d.). A-Z Quotes. https://www.azquotes.com/quote/138701

Day of the dead. (2018, October 30). History; A&E Television Networks. https://www.history.com/topics/halloween/day-of-the-dead

De Cruz, H. (2017, January 17). *Religion and science*. Stanford Encyclopedia of Philosophy. https://plato.stanford.edu/entries/religion-science/

Degenaar, M., & Lokhorst, G.-J. (2017). *Molyneux's problem* (E. N. Zalta, Ed.). Stanford Encyclopedia of Philosophy; Metaphysics Research Lab, Stanford University. https://plato.stanford.edu/entries/molyneux-problem/

Eshleman, A. (2019, October 16). *Moral responsibility*. Stanford Encyclopedia of Philosophy. https://plato.stanford.edu/entries/moral-responsibility/

Eternalism and its ethical implications. (n.d.). Reducing Suffering. https://reducing-suffering.org/eternalism-and-its-ethical-implications/

Evans, C. S. (2018). *Moral arguments for the existence of god* (E. N. Zalta, Ed.). Stanford Encyclopedia of Philosophy; Metaphysics Research Lab, Stanford University. https://plato.stanford.edu/entries/moral-arguments-god/#PraMorArgForBelGod

Fayard, J. V. (2021, September 29). *Do people with amnesia know if their personality has changed?* Psychology Today Canada. https://www.psychologytoday.com/ca/blog/people-are-strange/202109/do-people-amnesia-know-if-their-personality-has-changed

Fischler, J. (2022, June 30). *History made: Ketanji Brown Jackson sworn in as U.S. Supreme Court justice*. Louisiana Illuminator. https://lailluminator.com/2022/06/30/history-made-ketanji-brown-jackson-sworn-in-as-u-s-supreme-court-justice/

Ford, F. M. (1915). *The good soldier: A tale of passion*. John Lane, The Bodley Head.

Forrest, P. (2017). *The epistemology of religion* (E. N. Zalta, Ed.). Stanford Encyclopedia of Philosophy; Metaphysics Research Lab, Stanford University. https://plato.stanford.edu/entries/religion-epistemology/

Foy, R. (2019, March 12). *What is method acting?* The Lee Strasberg Theatre & Film Institute. https://strasberg.edu/about/what-is-method-acting/

Free will and moral responsibility. (2019a). UCL. https://www.ucl.ac.uk/~uctytho/dfwFischer2.html

Free will and moral responsibility. (2019b, April 22). 1000-Word Philosophy: An Introductory Anthology. https://1000wordphilosophy.com/2014/06/02/free-will-and-moral-responsibility/

Grudin, R. (2019). *Humanism: Definition, principles, history, & influence*. Encyclopædia Britannica. https://www.britannica.com/topic/humanism

Happiness: What is it to be happy? (2021, May 8). 1000-Word Philosophy: An Introductory Anthology. https://1000wordphilosophy.com/2021/05/08/happiness/

Haybron, D. (2011). *Happiness*. Stanford Encyclopedia of Philosophy. https://plato.stanford.edu/entries/happiness/

How colours matter to philosophy. (n.d.). Notre Dame Philosophical Reviews. https://ndpr.nd.edu/reviews/how-colours-matter-to-philosophy/

How long is right now? Calculating the present. (n.d.). Vice. https://www.vice.com/en/article/qjd4yd/how-long-is-right-now

Hugo, V. (1862). *Les misérables*. A. Lacroix, Verboeckhoven & Cie.

Hyde, D., & Raffman, D. (2018). *Sorites paradox*. Stanford Encyclopedia of Philosophy. https://plato.stanford.edu/entries/sorites-paradox/

Immanuel Kant quote. (n.d.). A-Z Quotes. https://www.azquotes.com/quote/152871

Immortality. (n.d.). Internet Encyclopedia of Philosophy. https://iep.utm.edu/immortal/

Is color a property of matter or generated in our brain? (2017, November 19). Science ABC. https://www.scienceabc.com/eyeopeners/is-color-a-property-of-matter-or-generated-in-our-brain.html

Is death bad? Epicurus and Lucretius on the fear of death. (2020, October 2). 1000-Word Philosophy: An Introductory Anthology. https://1000wordphilosophy.com/2020/10/02/is-death-bad/

Is immortality desirable? (2020, January 23). 1000-Word Philosophy: An Introductory Anthology. https://1000wordphilosophy.com/2020/01/23/is-immortality-desirable/

Johnston, S. I. (2017). Many (un)happy returns: Ancient Greek concepts of a return from death and their later counterparts. *Coming back to Life*, 17–36. https://comingbacktolife.library.mcgill.ca/article/view/8/51

Lazarus, C. N. (2020). *Why time goes by faster as we age*. Psychology Today Canada. https://www.psychologytoday.com/ca/blog/thinkwell/202011/why-time-goes-faster-we-age#:~:text=Bejan%20hypothesizes%20that%2C%20over%20time

Levin, N. (2021, January 18). *Ship of Theseus*. Tulsa Community College. https://open.library.okstate.edu/introphilosophy/chapter/ship-of-theseus/

Linklater, R. (Director). (2004). *Before sunset* [Film]. Warner Independent Pictures.

Livni, E. (2017, April 6). *Kokoro, a Japanese word connecting mind, body, and spirit is also driving scientific discovery*. Quartz. https://qz.com/946438/kokoro-a-japanese-word-connecting-mind-body-and-spirit-is-also-driving-scientific-discovery

Luper, S. (2019). *Death*. Stanford Encyclopedia of Philosophy. https://plato.stanford.edu/entries/death/

Martin, G. R. R. (1996). *A game of thrones*. Bantam Spectra.

Maund, B. (2018). *Color*. Stanford Encyclopedia of Philosophy. https://plato.stanford.edu/entries/color/

McLeod, S. (2018). *Erik Erikson's stages of psychosocial development*. Simply Psychology. https://www.simplypsychology.org/Erik-Erikson.html#identity

Metz, T. (2007, May 15). *The meaning of life*. Stanford Encyclopedia of Philosophy. https://plato.stanford.edu/entries/life-meaning/

Mitchell, J. (2021, August 15). *240 philosophical questions for deep critical thinking & debate*. Homeschool Adventure. https://homeschooladventure.com/blog/philosophical-questions/

Molyneux's question. (n.d.). Internet Encyclopedia of Philosophy. https://iep.utm.edu/molyneux/

Moore, Andrew, "Hedonism", *The Stanford Encyclopedia of Philosophy* (Winter 2019 Edition), Edward N. Zalta (ed.). https://plato.stanford.edu/archives/win2019/entries/hedonism/

Moral luck. (2014, May 8). 1000-Word Philosophy: An Introductory Anthology. https://1000wordphilosophy.com/2014/05/08/moral-luck/

Morley, B. (n.d.). *Western concepts of God*. Internet Encyclopedia of Philosophy. https://iep.utm.edu/god-west/

Münchhausen trilemma: Is it possible to prove any truth? (2020, February 26). Science ABC. https://www.scienceabc.com/social-science/munchhausens-trilemma-is-it-possible-to-prove-any-truth.html

Navajo Burial Customs and Fear of the Dead. (n.d.). AAANativearts.com. https://www.aaanativearts.com/navajo-burial-customs-and-fear-of-the-dead

Nelson Goodman quote. (n.d.). A-Z Quotes. https://www.azquotes.com/quote/1050204

Nolan, C. (Director). (2000). *Memento* [Film]. Summit Entertainment.

Olson, E. T. (2019). *Personal identity* (E. N. Zalta, Ed.). Stanford Encyclopedia of Philosophy; Metaphysics Research Lab, Stanford University. https://plato.stanford.edu/entries/identity-personal/#Fis

Ostberg, René. "transhumanism". Encyclopedia Britannica, 3 Nov. 2022, https://www.britannica.com/topic/transhumanism

Panahi, O. (2016). *Could there be a solution to the trolley problem?* Philosophy Now. https://philosophynow.org/issues/116/Could_There_Be_A_Solution_To_The_Trolley_Problem

People Feared Being Buried Alive So Much They Invented These Special Safety Coffins. Smithsonian Magazine. https://www.smithsonianmag.com/sponsored/people-feared-being-buried-alive-so-much-they-invented-these-special-safety-coffins-180970627/

Philosophy of space and time: Are the past and future real? (2022, June 24). 1000-Word Philosophy: An Introductory Anthology. https://1000wordphilosophy.com/2022/06/24/philosophy-of-time/

Plato. (2007). *The republic* (D. Lee, Trans.). Penguin Classics. (Original work published ca. 375 B.C.E.).

Plato. (2014). *Theaetetus* (B. Jowett, Trans.). CreateSpace Independent Publishing Platform. (Original work published ca. 369 B.C.E.).

Plato quote. (n.d.). A-Z Quotes. https://www.azquotes.com/quote/668186

Popkin, R. H. (2017). *Skepticism.* Encyclopædia Britannica. https://www.britannica.com/topic/skepticism

Problem of the criterion. (n.d.). Internet Encyclopedia of Philosophy. https://iep.utm.edu/problem-of-the-criterion/

The problem of induction. (n.d.). PH100: Problems of Philosophy. https://scholarblogs.emory.edu/millsonph100/2014/11/03/the-problem-of-induction/

The problem of induction. (2014, May 26). 1000-Word Philosophy: An Introductory Anthology. https://1000wordphilosophy.com/2014/05/26/the-problem-of-induction/

Propst, J. (2021, November 22). *Culture and Death: Native American Heritage.* Alive Hospice. https://www.alivehospice.org/news-events/culture-and-death-native-american-heritage/

Psychological approaches to personal identity: Do memories and consciousness make us who we are? (2022, February 3). 1000-Word Philosophy: An Introductory Anthology. https://1000wordphilosophy.com/2022/02/03/psychological-approaches-to-personal-identity/

Salinger, J. D. (1951). *The catcher in the rye.* Little, Brown and Company.

Saving the many or the few: The moral relevance of numbers. (2022, October 9). 1000-Word Philosophy: An Introductory Anthology. https://1000wordphilosophy.com/2022/10/09/saving-the-many-or-the-few/

Scott, J., Scott, J., & Scott, J. (2022, November 22). *Top 10 Superheroes That Can Time Travel (Marvel and DC).* Comic Basics. https://www.comicbasics.com/superheroes-that-can-time-travel/

Shakespeare, W. (2019). *To be or not to be, Hamlet.* Poetry Foundation. https://www.poetryfoundation.org/poems/56965/speech-to-be-or-not-to-be-that-is-the-question

Siegel, E. (2022, October 14). *Ask Ethan: Is our Universe a hologram?* Big Think. Retrieved January 3, 2023, from https://bigthink.com/starts-with-a-bang/universe-hologram/

Socrates quote. (n.d.). A-Z Quotes. https://www.azquotes.com/quote/670336

Sophocles. (1990). *Antigone* (R. E. Braun, Trans.). Oxford University Press. (Original work published ca. 441 B.C.E.).

Soren Kierkegaard quote. (2019). A-Z Quotes. https://www.azquotes.com/quote/158106

Sorensen, R. (2017). *Nothingness.* Stanford Encyclopedia of Philosophy. https://plato.stanford.edu/entries/nothingness/

Soyinka, W. (1975). *Death and the king's horseman.* W. W. Norton & Company

Stephen, E. C. (2014). *Moral arguments for the existence of God.* Stanford Encyclopedia of Philosophy. https://plato.stanford.edu/entries/moral-arguments-god/

Steps of the scientific method. (n.d.). Science Buddies. https://www.sciencebuddies.org/science-fair-projects/science-fair/steps-of-the-scientific-method#:~:text=The%20six%20steps%20of%20the%20scientific%20method%20include%3A%201

Strickland, L. (n.d.). *Answering the biggest question of all: Why is there something rather than nothing?* The Conversation. https://theconversation.com/answering-the-biggest-question-of-all-why-is-there-something-rather-than-nothing-65865

Tardi, C. (2020, June 14). *Utilitarianism defined.* Investopedia. https://www.investopedia.com/terms/u/utilitarianism.asp#:~:text=Utilitarianism%20is%20a%20theory%20of

The Australian Museum. (n.d.). *Safety coffins.* https://australian.museum/about/history/exhibitions/death-the-last-taboo/safety-coffins/

The Gettier problem & the definition of knowledge. (2014, April 10). 1000-Word Philosophy: An Introductory Anthology. https://1000wordphilosophy.com/2014/04/10/the-gettier-problem/

The mind-body problem. (n.d.). Spot.colorado.edu. https://spot.colorado.edu/~heathwoo/Phil100/mindintro.html

The Jellyfish That Never Dies. (n.d.). BBC Earth. https://www.bbcearth.com/news/the-jellyfish-that-never-dies

Vitalism. (n.d.). Encyclopedia Britannica. https://www.britannica.com/topic/vitalism

Westphal, J. (2019, August 8). *Descartes and the discovery of the mind-body problem.* The MIT Press Reader. https://thereader.mitpress.mit.edu/discovery-mind-body-problem/

What Does a Bee See. (n.d.). Mann Lake Bee & Ag Supply. https://www.-mannlakeltd.com/blog/what-does-a-bee-see/

What Does 42 Mean? (2018, March 1). Dictionary.com. https://www.dictionary.-com/e/slang/42/

What is "Kokoro"? A meaning beyond 'heart' or "spirit." (2022, July 13). Kokoro Media. https://kokoro-jp.com/what-is-kokoro/

Wole Soyinka, death and the king's horseman. (n.d.). Harvard Wiki. https://wiki.harvard.edu/confluence/pages/viewpage.action?pageId=164234929

Worley, G. G. (n.d.). *The problem of the criterion.* Lesswrong. https://www.lesswrong.com/posts/Xs7ag4gsiA6zspmsD/the-problem-of-the-criterion

Young, L. J. (n.d.). *This community in Sulawesi, Indonesia keeps the dead in homes for years.* Inverse. https://www.inverse.com/article/13380-this-community-in-sulawesi-indonesia-keeps-the-dead-in-homes-for-years

Zygon Journal of Religion and Science, & Tirosh-Samuelson, H. (2012, November 20). *Transhumanism as a Secularist Faith.* Wiley Online Library. https://onlinelibrary.wiley.com/doi/abs/10.1111/j.1467-9744.2012.01288.x

Only the past is real. According to neuroscientist, the brain ~~takes~~ takes a second to process what we see before us. Therefore, if we see an action, by the time our brain has seen it a second has past. So the act has gone since ~~the~~ we have seen it; that means the act is not in the present but in the past. This leads to the statement that only the past is real. Complex and baffling.

Printed in Great Britain
by Amazon